Guangdong Operational Guidelines for Administrators

Lin Lu, Zhendong Li

Copyright © 2023 Dean & Francis Press

All rights reserved. No part of this publication may be reproduced, distributed, or transmitted in any form or by any means, including photocopying, recording, or other electronic or mechanical methods, without the prior written permission of the publisher, except in the case of brief quotations embodied in critical reviews and certain other noncommercial uses permitted by copyright law.

Title: Guangdong Operational Guidelines for Administrators
Author: Lin Lu, Zhendong Li
Edition: 1 Edition

ISBN: 979-8-89120-004-3

Published by Dean & Francis Press
201 E Center ST STE
Anatheim, CA, 92805
acceptance@deanfrancispress.com

Printing History: None
First Printing: June, 2023

Legal Disclaimers:

The copyright of this book belongs to Dean & Francis, and no one is allowed to use it without compensation. If you need to use it, please contact the official email address. Only after approval can it be used for academic or commercial purposes.

Trademarks:

Indicate any trademarks included in the book and state the ownership of those trademarks belongs to the author and Dean & Francis Press.

Editorial Board

Practice Guidelines for Bankruptcy Administrators in Guangdong Province

Editor-in-chief: Zhu Zhengfu

Associate editors: Hu Minshan; Lu Lin; Han Zhenping

Members: Chen Liangjun; Li Zhendong; Dong Shuo; Lu Shangjun; Zheng Feihu; Chen Lianshu; Zhang Xiaoling; Liu Lihua; Wang Lihai; Tan Ling; Cui Feng; Wang Zilong; Lai Xiangdong; Tan Rixing; Du Chenhua; Liang Yv; Deng Peiqi; Song Wei; Chen Dong; Gao Chao; Xie Lanjun; Liu Kaitan; Xiang Hengxiang; Tang Wen; Zeng Lixia; Xin Zhiqi

Guangdong Operational Guidelines for Administrators

Editor-in-chief: Lu lin; Li Zhendong

Associate editors: Dong Shuo; Lu Shangjun; Wang Xuedan; Jin Yv

Members: Chen Liangjun; Zheng Feihu; Cui Feng;Tang Wen; Wang Lihai; Tan Ling; Zeng Lixia; Liang Bin; Yang Zhenyv; Kang Lingli; Zhou Junwei; Wang Wei; Xiang Hengxiang; Zhang Xiaoling; Xin Zhiqi; Xiao Xiaojun; Zou Yang; Liu Kaitan; He Ying; Chen Lianshu

Notification on the Promulgation of Guangdong Operational Guidelines for Administrators (Trial)

Dear Members,

With the purpose to help our Members to improve their performance of duties as administrators, and encourage them to perform such duties diligently and faithfully, the Guangdong Operational Guidelines for Bankruptcy Administrators (for trial implementation) are developed under the aegis of the Association. These Guidelines, which have been prepared upon consulting the People's Courts in Guangdong and adopted at the Association's Chairmen Meeting and by the Expert Committee upon deliberation, are hereby issued in their full length. All Members are requested to organize their team members to first earnestly study the guidelines and then perform their duties in line herewith, taking into account the professional practice of the administrators. Should you encounter any problems or difficulties in the implementation hereof, timely feedback to the Association is most welcome.

the Guangdong Association of Bankruptcy Administrators
November 26, 2021

Contents

Chapter I General Provisions 1

    Section 1 Purpose and Special Reminders 1
    Section 2 Withdrawal, Resignation and Replacement of
                 Administrators 2
    Section 3 Basic Obligations of the Administrator......................6
    Section 4 Business System and Working Mechanism of
                 the Administrator 8
    Section 5 Management of Bankruptcy Case Files 10

Chapter II Enterprise Liquidation 13

    Section 1 General Provisions 13
    Section 2 Obtaining Seals and Opening Bank Accounts 14
    Section 3 Takeover of the Debtor 16
    Section 4 Investigation of the Assets of the Debtor 23
    Section 5 Managing the Internal Affairs of the Debtor 30
    Section 6 Management of the Debtor's Assets 33
    Section 7 Registration and Inspection of Claims 45
    Section 8 Convening of Creditors' Meetings 53
    Section 9 Representing the Debtor in Actions, Arbitration or
                 Other Legal Proceedings 56
    Section 10 Realization of Assets in Bankruptcy 58
    Section 11 Distribution of Assets in Bankruptcy 60
    Section 12 Placing of Certain Assets in Bankruptcy in
                 Escrow and Its Announcement 63
    Section 13 Termination of the Administrator's Duties 64

Section 14　Special Provisions on the Cases Transferred from Enforcement to Bankruptcy Proceedings and the Summary Proceedings 66

Chapter III　Compulsory Liquidation **70**

Section 1　General Provisions 70
Section 2　Scope of Work of a Liquidation team 72
Section 3　Execution and Termination of a Liquidation Plan......... 78

Chapter IV　Individual Bankruptcy **80**

Section 1　Selection and Appointment of Administrators 80
Section 2　Investigation of the Debtor's Assets 81
Section 3　Taking over and Disposing of the Debtor's Assets 85
Section 4　Representing the Debtor in Actions, Arbitration or Other Legal Proceedings 88
Section 5　Handling of Special Circumstances Occurred to the Debtor 89
Section 6　Duties to Supervise the Debtor 90
Section 7　Other Provisions 92

Chapter V　Reorganization **93**

Section 1　General Provisions 93
Section 2　Managing the Debtor's Assets and Business Affairs...... 94
Section 3　Self-Management of the Debtor's Assets and Business Affairs..101
Section 4　Consolidated Reorganization of Related Debtor Companies...107
Section 5　Reorganization Investors 111
Section 6　Preparation, Adoption and Approval of the Reorganization Plan 114
Section 7　Debt-for-Equity Swap 122
Section 8　Implementation of a Reorganization Plan..................124
Section 9　Termination of Reorganization Proceedings...............129

Chapter VI Pre-reorganization 131

Section 1 General Provisions 131
Section 2 Duties of the Administrator for Pre-reorganization 132
Section 3 Preparation and Adoption of a Draft
           Pre-reorganization Plan 136
Section 4 Termination of Pre-reorganization 137
Section 5 Connection of Pre-reorganization and
           Reorganization Procedures 139
Section 6 Pre-reorganization Administrator Remuneration and
           Pre-reorganization Expenses 141

Chapter VII Composition 143

Section 1 General Provisions 143
Section 2 Initiation of Composition Proceedings 144
Section 3 Implementation of the Composition Proceedings 146
Section 4 Termination of Composition Proceedings..................148
Section 5 Handling of Failed Composition 150

Chapter VIII Cross-border Insolvency 151

Section 1 Guidelines for Mainland Work of
           Hong Kong Managers 151
Section 2 Guidelines for Overseas Work of Domestic
           Administrators 159

Chapter IX Bankruptcy Audit 162

Section 1 Concept and Scope of Bankruptcy Audit 162
Section 2 Debtor's Property Check 163
Section 3 Inspection and Review of Bankruptcy Claims 166
Section 4 Specific Behavior Audit 169
Section 5 Economic Calculation 172

Chapter X Bankruptcy-Related Tax Matters 175

Chapter XI Supplementary Provisions.................................177

Chapter I General Provisions

Section 1 Purpose and Special Reminders

Article 1 Purpose

These Operational Guidelines are developed, upon taking into account the hands-on experience accumulated in Guangdong Province and other areas, in accordance with the Civil Code of the People's Republic of China (hereinafter referred to as the "Civil Code"), the Enterprise Bankruptcy Law of the People's Republic of China (hereinafter referred to as the "Enterprise Bankruptcy Law"), the Company Law of the People's Republic of China (hereinafter referred to as the "Company Law") and the provisions of other relevant laws, administrative regulations and judicial interpretations. The guidelines aim to guide the administrators of Guangdong in handling bankruptcy and compulsory liquidation cases and regulate their practice so that they can deliver better services and avoid professional risks. Also, they intend to allow the administrators to fully play their critical role in the aforementioned cases.

Article 2 Effects and applicability

The Operational Guidelines serve as guiding opinions for Members acting as bankruptcy administrators and/or liquidation team members. Members shall perform their duties and responsibilities in line with the Guidelines.

Article 3 Application of bankruptcy liquidation rules to compulsory liquidation

A Member, when acting as a liquidation team member to handle compulsory liquidation, shall do so pursuant to the relevant provisions of Chapters I and II hereof, unless otherwise provided for in Chapter III.

Section 2 Withdrawal, Resignation and Replacement of Administrators

Article 4 Withdrawal on one's initiative

Where a Member, after being appointed as an administrator by the People's Court (hereinafter referred to as the "Court"), finds himself having, as set out in the Enterprise Bankruptcy Law and relevant judicial interpretations, "an interest in the case" or under "other circumstances where an individual or entity may be deemed by the Court as unfit for the role of administrator", the Member shall file with the Court to withdraw from or refuse the appointment with explanations.

While competing for the job of administrator publicly posted by the Court, a Member shall report to the Court on his own initiative if he finds himself in any circumstance prescribed in the first paragraph of this article.

Article 5 Other circumstances where an individual or entity is considered unfit for the role of administrator

An Institutional Member appointed as an administrator by the Court shall be considered under "other circumstances where an individual or entity may be deemed by the Court as unfit for the role of administrator" as stipulated in Subparagraph 4, Paragraph 3, Article 24 of the Enterprise Bankruptcy Law, and the relevant judicial interpretations, if the Member is in any of the situations below:

(i) Three years have not elapsed since the imposition of administrative penalty or discipline on the Member by any administrative, regulatory authorities or industrial self-regulatory organization, owing to intentional or gross negligence in practice related to bankruptcy or liquidation;

(ii) The Member is being investigated by the competent authorities due to suspected illegal acts committed in the practice related to bankruptcy or liquidation, or due to criminal acts;

(iii) His practicing or business license is revoked or cancelled;

(iv) Three years have not elapsed since the Member's removal from the register of administrators by the Court, due to improper performance of his duties, or refusal to accept the appointment of the Court without any justification, among others;

(v) The Member is not included in the list of administrators kept by the Court or fails to meet the requirements for the level of administrator required by the type of a case;

(vi) The Member lacks civil capacity;

(vii) The Member is included in the blacklist of dishonest persons subject to enforcement;

(viii) The Member faces problems that may lead to his dissolution or bankruptcy, or loses the capacity to assume professional liability risks;

(ix) The Member has a history of harming the interests of creditors due to his intentional or gross negligence in the performance of the administrator's duties;

(x) Other circumstances that the People's Court considers may affect the performance of the administrator's duties.

An Individual Member appointed as an administrator by the Court shall be considered, as set out in the preceding paragraph, under "other circumstances where an individual or entity may be deemed by the Court as unfit for the role of administrator", if the member is in any of the situations listed below:

(i) His practicing qualification is cancelled or revoked;

(ii) Three years have not elapsed since the imposition of administrative penalty or discipline on the Member by any administrative, regulatory authorities or industrial self-regulatory organization, owing to intentional or gross negligence in practice related to bankruptcy or liquidation;

(iii) The Member has a history of causing serious harm to the interests of creditors due to his intentional or gross negligence in the performance of the administrator's duties;

(iv) Three years have not elapsed since the Member's removal from the register of administrators by the People's Court, due to improper performance of his duties, or refusal to accept the appointment of the People's Court without any justification, among others;

(v) The Member lacks civil capacity;

(vi) The Member is missing, dead or incapacitated for civil acts;

(vii) The Member is unable to execute his office due to health issues;

(viii) His insurance against professional liability becomes invalid;

(ix) The Member is included in the blacklist of dishonest persons subject to enforcement;

(x) The Member is being investigated by the competent authorities due to suspected illegal acts committed in the practice related to bankruptcy or liquidation;

(xi) Other circumstances that the Court considers may affect the performance of the administrator's duties.

Article 6 Application, *mutatis mutandis*, of the provisions on the circumstances where an individual is deemed unqualified for the post of an administrator

If any person dispatched by an Institutional Member, acting in the capacity of administrator, is found to be in any of the circumstances specified in Article 5 hereof, which may affect the faithful performance of the administrator's duties, it shall be deemed to fall under the circumstances listed in Subparagraph (4), Paragraph 3, Article 24 of the Enterprise Bankruptcy Law.

"Person dispatched" under this article include: (a) the administrator team members, and the field and on-site staff appointed by the Institutional Member who has been designated by the People's Court to act as the administrator, and (b) the staff entrusted by the administrator with relevant investigation work and some of his duties.

Article 7 Replacement of administrators

After the appointment of an administrator by the People's Court, if the creditors' meeting requests the Court to replace the administrator, the administrator shall explain in time as required by the Court.

The administrator, prior to the decision of the People's Court to replace him with a new administrator, shall continue to perform his duties according to law.

Article 8 Handover of duties from the replaced administrator to the new one

If a Member appointed as an administrator by the People's Court: (a) applies to the court for withdrawal or resignation according to law and such application is approved by the Court, or (b) the Court decides to replace the administrator at the request of the creditors' meeting, the member shall stop performing his duties as an administrator from the date of the appointment of a new administrator. Further, he shall, under the supervision of the Court, hand over to the new administrator the data, assets and business affairs under his charge, state his work progress timely in writing, and respond, at any time before the conclusion of the bankruptcy proceedings, to the inquiries raised by the new administrator, the creditors' meeting and the Court regarding the duties that he has already performed.

Section 3　Basic Obligations of the Administrator

Article 9　Obligation of faithfulness

The administrator shall uphold professional ethics. He shall perform his duties diligently and faithfully, and treat all creditors, debtors and stakeholders in a fair and impartial manner. Also, he shall not use his position or power to seek illegitimate benefits.

Article 10　Obligation of diligence

The administrator shall work efficiently to save on expenses incurred from the bankruptcy process.

The administrator shall always follow the prudence principle. He shall handle relevant affairs in accordance with law to effectively hedge against legal risks.

Article 11　Obligation to timely report

The administrator shall timely report his work to the People's Court and be subject to the supervision by the creditors' meeting and the creditors' committee.

The administrator shall attend the creditors' meetings as a non-voting participant, reporting on the performance of his duties and answering inquires.

Article 12　Obligation of strict confidentiality

The administrator shall strictly perform the confidentiality obligation. The administrator shall hold in confidence the information obtained while doing his job as an administrator, including state secrets, the trade secrets and personal privacy of the debtors, creditors and other interested parties, and other matters that cannot be disclosed to the public.

Article 13　Obligation to perform duties in person

The administrator shall personally perform his duties. He shall not transfer, in any form, all or part of his duties to any other organization or individual without prior consent of the People's Court.

Article 14 Obligation not to resign willfully

An administrator shall not refuse the appointment made by the Court or resign from his post without any justification. He may resign from the post only upon approval by the Court.

Article 15 Basic duties of an administrator

A Member acting as an administrator shall perform the following duties.

(i) Taking over the assets, seals, account books and documents of the debtor;

(ii) Investigate the assets of the debtor and preparing the relevant financial statements;

(iii) Deciding on the internal management affairs of the debtor;

(iv) Deciding on the overheads and other necessary expenditures of the debtor;

(v) Deciding, prior to the convening of the first creditors' meeting, whether to continue or cease the debtor's business;

(vi) Managing and disposing of the debtors' assets;

(vii) Participating in actions, arbitration or any other legal procedures on behalf of the debtor;

(viii) Proposing to convene creditors' meetings; and

(ix) Performing any other duties that the People's Court holds the administrator shall perform.

Where the duties of the administrator are otherwise provided in relevant laws and judicial interpretations, such provisions shall apply.

Section 4 Business System and Working Mechanism of the Administrator

Article 16 Work System of the Administrator

The administrator shall, within seven working days upon receipt of the People's Court decision to appoint him as the administrator, draw up a relevant work system, including the code of practice, rules of procedure at meetings, financial revenue and expenditure management system, certification and seal management system, emergency contingency plans, file management system, and confidential rules and regulations. The said system shall be implemented after being filed with the People's Court.

Article 17 Internal management system of the administrator

Members included into the list of administrators published by the People's Court shall, in light of their own actual conditions, formulate relevant management systems, in case they may be appointed as administrators.

Such a management system generally encompasses:

(i) Administrator team composition and division of responsibilities;

(ii) Professional training system for administrators;

(iii) Business processing system for administrators;

(iv) Original working manuscript and file management system for administrators, and

(v) Compensation distribution and risk assumption system for administrators.

Article 18 The administrator's insurance against professional liability

Individual Members included in the list of administrators published by the People's Court shall purchase insurance against professional liability. Institutional Members shall decide for or against purchase of the said insurance in view of their own situations.

Article 19 Work plan of the administrator

After accepting the appointment by the People's Court, the administrator shall, in order to effectively perform his duties, provide a work plan based on the acquired specifics of the bankruptcy case and file the plan with the Court.

Article 20 Contents of the work plan for administrators

The work plan for administrators generally includes:

(i) Specific duties required to be performed by an administrator in a bankruptcy case;

(ii) Members of the administrator team assigned to perform the duties and their contact information;

(iii) Person in charge and specific division of labor among the team members;

(iv) A plan to take over the debtor's business;

(v) The timelines, ideas, steps and procedures for completing each work plan;

(vi) Plans for hiring relevant persons and other professional institutions, and the remuneration of administrators;

(vii) Budgeting for the administrator to carry out his duties; and

(viii) Measures to manage the professional risks of administrators.

The work plan should be comprehensive, complete, practical and feasible. The administrator may modify the work plan, if necessary, according to the progress of the work. The person in charge of the administrator team shall, as necessitated by work, convene and preside at the administrator's meetings, and may invite the judges of the People's Court and the legal representative of the debtor and other relevant persons to attend the meetings where necessary.

Section 5 Management of Bankruptcy Case Files

Article 21 Bankruptcy case files

The administrator shall keep relevant files while handling bankruptcy cases.

"Bankruptcy case files" refer to the work records kept and the necessary materials obtained by the administrator while handling enterprise bankruptcy cases, which will serve as the critical grounds for judging whether the administrator is doing his job legally, diligently and responsibly. Such files kept by the administrator shall reflect the truth relating to the bankruptcy proceedings in a timely, accurate, comprehensive and objective manner.

Article 22 Basic requirements for bankruptcy case files

Bankruptcy case files shall be complete with clear and unequivocal conclusion, and shall be marked with index and serial numbers.

The said files shall be originals developed in the course of doing the administrator's work. If copies are used, their original sources shall be indicated.

Article 23 Contents of bankruptcy case files

Bankruptcy case files generally include the following:

(i) Documents presented at the time when a bankruptcy application is filed before the People's Court, including the application filed by the creditor or debtor, statements of the debtor's assets, inventory of debts, inventory of creditor's claims, financial and accounting reports, statements of employee placement, previous tax declaration and payment, as well as payment of social insurance premiums;

(ii) The civil ruling of the Court accepting the bankruptcy case, the Court decision to appoint the administrator and relevant legal documents issued by the Court to the administrator;

(iii) Internal work plan for the administrator team, relevant rules and regulations, composition and work division of the administrator group members, and documents issued by the administrator to other organizations;

(iv) Materials about the administrator's taking over and investigation of the debtor's assets, business affairs, seals, account books and documents;

(v) Documents for filing and verification of claims, which include claims filing paper and forms, evidentiary materials, proof of capital flow, grounds for examination and the conclusions;

(vi) The administrator shall investigate the employment contracts, payment of salary and social insurance premiums, and other materials related to the debtor's labor claims, as well as the documents in connection with the announcement of, objection against and correction of such claims;

(vii) The administrator's work plan and records of its execution. Records of communication and meetings between the administrator and the relevant persons of the debtor; records of examination, investigation and review of the materials provided by the debtor; correspondence, on-site investigation records, lists of documents consulted and other relevant information and detailed statements;

(viii) Litigation documents and relevant materials used while the administrator represents the debtor in litigation, arbitration or other legal proceedings;

(ix) Notices, agendas, documents and minutes of creditors' meetings, voting results and other relevant materials;

(x) Materials presented to the People's Court, creditors' meetings and the creditors' committee;

(xi) Other materials involved in the performance of the administrator's duties.

The source of the above-mentioned materials shall be indicated. Any record of the investigation made by the administrator into a party concerned shall be signed by the party and two or more members of the administrator team.

Article 24 Maintenance of bankruptcy case files

The administrator shall, in a timely and accurate manner, prepare the bankruptcy case files and other relevant documents, and properly keep them. The administrator, if failing to do so, shall bear the liabilities accordingly.

The administrator shall incorporate the handling of bankruptcy case files into the bankruptcy work procedure. The costs required for the filing, storage, digital processing, transfer and destruction of such files may be disbursed from the bankruptcy expenses to ensure an orderly handling of the files.

Chapter II Enterprise Liquidation

Section 1 General Provisions

Article 25 Office term of a bankruptcy liquidation administrator

The office term of an administrator in the bankruptcy liquidation proceedings commences from the time when the People's Court appoints him as the administrator and ends the next day upon the completion of the debtor's deregistration. However, this does not apply to the circumstance where there is a pending litigation or arbitration.

If, after the People's Court accepts a application for bankruptcy liquidation, the court decides, to reject the application or to terminate the bankruptcy proceedings before the debtor is declared bankrupt. The office term of the administrator shall begin at the time of the court appointment and expires when the People's Court decision becomes legally effective.

If, after the People's Court accepts the application for bankruptcy liquidation, the court decides, before the debtor is declared bankrupt, that the debtor is to be reorganized or reconcile with creditors and therefore a new administrator is appointed, the office term of the original administrator starts at the time of his appointment as administrator and expires at the time of the appointment of the new administrator. Where the original administrator continues to serve as the administrator after the People's Court orders the debtor to reorganize or reconcile, his office term shall begin at the time of his appointment as an administrator, and expire as determined in accordance with the relevant laws, judicial interpretations and the provisions hereof concerning reorganization or composition procedures.

Section 2 Obtaining Seals and Opening Bank Accounts

Article 26 Obtaining a seal for the administrator

After accepting the appointment by the People's Court, the administrator may bring the following documents and have his seal made by a business eligible to carve common seals upon approval of public security organs: the Court decision to accept the bankruptcy application, the Court decision to appoint the administrator, a letter to the public security organ requesting to obtain a seal of the administrator, copies of ID card of the person in charge of the administrator as appointed by the Court (original ID shall be presented for checking), letter of the administrator's organization, identity certificate and copies of ID card of the legal representative (person in charge) of the administrator's organization, as well as other materials required by the local public security organ.

Article 27 Use of the administrator's seal

The administrator, upon obtaining his seal, shall file the seal sample with the People's Court for record, and may use it thereafter. The seal shall be used only in the execution of the administrator's duties. The administrator shall devise a seal management system and use the seal accordingly.

Article 28 Opening an administrator's account

The administrator, after obtaining his seal, may apply to the bank for opening an account for himself by presenting the People's Court decision to accept the bankruptcy application, the Court decision to appoint the administrator, his identity certificate and other documentation.

Where the administrator finds it unnecessary to open an account, due to the debtor's absence of assets, he may not apply for opening an account for the time being.

Article 29 Use of the Administrator's Account

The administrator, upon the opening of his account, may transfer the bank deposits of the debtor into his account for unified management. In the event of failure of such transfer, the administrator may apply to the court for assisting the transfer. All receipts and expenditures, incurred by and from performing his duties according to law, shall be dealt with through using the administrator's account.

The administrator's account shall be used only in the execution of his duties. The administrator shall develop an account management system, and use the account accordingly under the supervision of the People's Court and the creditors' meeting.

The administrator shall apply to the court and the bank for extension of his account if, prior to the conclusion of the bankruptcy case, such an extension application is required by the bank for managerial reasons.

Section 3 Takeover of the Debtor

Article 30 Notification to creditors

The administrator shall, within twenty-five days upon the People's Court's acceptance of the bankruptcy application, assist the Court in notifying the known creditors in accordance with Article 14 of the Enterprise Bankruptcy Law, and announce the same to the public.

In cases of bankruptcies that are processed in an expedited procedure, the administrator shall, within seven days upon the receipt of his appointment, notify the known creditors to file their claims and inform them of the matters relevant to the application of expedited procedure.

"Known creditor" means a creditor with accessible contact information who is preliminarily determined, in line with the information provided by the debtor and the files of the case, to have rights to claim against the debtor.

The administrator may inquire about actions or enforcement involving the debtor through China Judgments Online and China Enforcement Information Disclosure Website.

Article 31 Notification to the debtor

The administrator shall, prior to the takeover of the debtor's assets, seals, account books, documents and other materials, inform the relevant persons of the debtor of the content and scope of the proposed takeover, request them to prepare for the handover, and inform them in writing of the legal liability to be assumed if they violate the handover obligations. He may also inform, when he deems it necessary, the relevant persons of the debtor and persons related to the takeover other than the debtor.

The administrator shall inform the debtor and the relevant persons in writing that the latter shall, from the service date of the People's Court decision to accept the bankuptcy application on the debtor until the conclusion of the bankruptcy proceedings, assume the obligations provided by Article 15, the Enterprise Bankruptcy Law. In the case that the administrator cannot notify the debtor, he shall make a public announcement.

Article 32 Cooperating in notifying the market regulatory authorities

After the People's Court decides to accept the bankruptcy application, the administrator shall, when necessary, cooperate with the Court to deliver the decision to the local market regulatory authorities where the debtor is registered, and file with the authorities for record of the debtor under bankruptcy or compulsory liquidation.

Article 33 Notification to the bank

The administrator shall, upon the People's Court decision to accept the bankruptcy application, cooperate with the Court to notify the debtor's bank to stop the payment from the debtor's account. The debtor's overheads and other necessary expenses shall be first reviewed and approved by the administrator and then notified to the bank.

Article 34 Notification to tax authorities

The administrator shall deliver the People's Court decision to accept the bankruptcy application to the authorities charged with responsibility for collection of tax from the debtor, timely communicate with the authorities about the debtor's tax and related matters, and inform them of the declaration of tax claims against the debtor.

Article 35 Notification to the competent social security authorities

The administrator shall notify the competent authorities, timely and in writing, to file social security claims against the debtor.

Article 36 Preparation for takeover

After accepting the appointment by the People's Court, the administrator shall promptly assign individuals to prepare to take over the debtor's assets, seals, account books, documents and other materials. The administrator may arrange persons to peruse files kept by the Court to get the basics about the bankruptcy case and to learn about the takeover from the relevant persons of the debtor.

During his term of office, the administrator shall be entitled to request the relevant persons of the debtor to cooperate in the liquidation efforts and answer inquiries truthfully.

Article 37 Developing a takeover plan

The administrator may formulate a plan for the takeover of the debtor's assets, seals, account books, documents and other materials, and take over the same according to such a plan.

Article 38 Items subject to the takeover

The items of the debtor that are subject to takeover by the administrator generally include:

(i) The tangible property of the debtor, including movables and immovables, and the relevant certificates of title;

(ii) The debtor's cash, negotiable securities, specimen seal impression for checking bank accounts, bank USB-shield, bank account password, and bank drafts;

(iii) Certificates of the debtor's intellectual property rights, external investment, franchise and other intangible assets;

(iv) The debtor's official seal, special seal for finance, special seal for contract, special seal for invoice, seal for customs declaration, personal seal of its legal representative and other seals;

(v) The debtor's business license, tax registration, account opening permit, certificate of seal filing, foreign exchange registration certificate, customs registration certificate, business qualification documents and other approval, permission or authorization documents in connection with the debtor's business;

(vi) The debtor's general and subsidiary ledgers, standing books, journals, accounting vouchers, important blank vouchers, accounting statements and other financial books, tax returns, documents to and from tax authorities like taxation notices and receipts of filing for taxation, tax payment receipts and other tax documents, as well as the audit and evaluation materials of the debtor;

(vii) Documents approving the establishment of the debtor, its articles of association, management system, list of shareholders, resolutions of its shareholders' meeting, Board of Directors and Board of Supervisors, and minutes of its internal meetings, among others;

(viii) Contracts/agreements concluded by the debtor and documents about its claims, debts and others relating thereto.

(ix) Litigation and arbitration involving the debtor and the relevant materials;

(x) The debtor's personnel archives;

(xi) The debtor's computer data and authorization codes;

(xii) The administrator shall also take over all the assets, seals, account books, documents and other materials not owned by the debtor but under its possession or control.

The administrator shall also take over the licenses, assets, seals, account books, documents and other materials of any branch of the debtor, if any.

(xiii) Other important materials of the debtor.

Article 39 Takeover method

The administrator may take over the debtor's assets, seals, account books, documents and other materials all at a time; but he may also, considering the actual situation, take over the same by batches with reasonable intervals.

Article 40 Material handover procedure

Where the administrator takes over the debtor's assets, seals, account books, documents and other materials, he shall go through the handover procedures with the relevant persons of the debtor, and sign the handover document and list jointly with the latter upon confirmation. If any of the aforementioned materials fails to be handed over in practice, such materials shall be indicated in the handover document or list, and the debtor or its relevant persons shall explain by presenting evidence and clues, where a transcript thereof should also be kept.

Article 41 Written notice of termination of employment contract

While taking over the debtor, the administrator may notify its employees in writing to terminate their employment contracts, if he determines, in his prudent discretion after considering all factors, that reorganization or composition is not an option for the debtor and therefore there is no need to continue the business operations of the debtor.

Article 42 Removal of protective measures

If the debtor's assets have been, prior to the People's Court acceptance of the bankruptcy application, placed under protective or enforcement measures in accordance with law, which have not been removed after the Court acceptance of the application, the administrator shall apply for removal of such measures according to law, so as to effectively take over the debtor's assets.

Where the administrator considers it necessary to request the People's Court, which has decided to accept the bankruptcy application, to notify the relevant entities to remove the protective measures or suspend the enforcement measures, the administrator shall file the same with the said Court.

If the relevant entities refuse to do so without justification or fail to give feedback within a reasonable period of time, the administrator may request the People's Court which accepts the bankruptcy case to coordinate with those entities to make it happen, and he may also report the same to its superior authorities.

Chapter II Enterprise Liquidation

Article 43 Application for compulsory takeover

If the relevant persons of the debtor or persons with interests in the bankruptcy case do not assist or even hinder the administrator's takeover work, the administrator shall report in writing to the People's Court and may request the Court to take necessary measures against the debtor or relevant entities, ordering the latter to assist in the takeover within a time limit. If the debtor or relevant entities and individuals still fail to perform the assistance obligation, the administrator may apply to the Court for compulsory execution by taking necessary measures, such as search and compulsory delivery, in accordance with the provisions on the enforcement procedure under the Civil Procedure Law of the PRC.

Article 44 Timely reporting to public security organ

Where the administrator finds, in the takeover process, that any relevant person of the debtor has concealed assets, falsely recorded the balance sheet or inventory of assets, or distributed the debtor's assets before the debts are paid off, he may report to the public security organ if the aforesaid acts may constitute a crime.

Where the administrator finds that any relevant person of the debtor has concealed or destroyed, deliberately, the accounting vouchers and books, and financial statements that shall be kept according to law, he may timely report the case to the public security organ if the offenses are serious. Where the administrator finds that any of the debtor's relevant persons has fabricated or destroyed pertinent evidentiary materials, or committed bankruptcy fraud by concealing assets, claiming false debts or transferring or disposing of assets by other means, he may report to the public security organ if such acts may constitute a crime.

The administrator shall report to the People's Court, and may also report to the public security organ if he finds, while liquidating the debtor's assets, that such assets have been looted or sold illegally by the debtor's creditors and other persons.

Article 45 Disappearance of the relevant persons of the debtor

Where the administrator is unable to take over the aforementioned materials, as a result of the unknown location of the relevant persons of the debtor or any other reason, the administrator shall continue to perform other duties and timely report the situation to the People's Court.

The "relevant persons of the debtor" refer to the individuals mentioned in Article 15, Paragraph 2 of the Enterprise Bankruptcy Law, which reads, "The relevant persons mentioned in the preceding paragraph refer to the debtor's legal representative, who may, upon decision by the People's Court, also include its financial and other executives."

The administrator shall, based on the identity information of the relevant persons obtained from the internal files kept by the competent industrial and commercial authorities, inform such persons in writing of the legal liability and consequences for failing to perform their legal obligations, and may make an announcement as needed.

The above-mentioned legal liability and consequences shall also be informed to the debtor's shareholders, contributors or competent authorities.

Article 46 Takeover report

Upon completion of the takeover, the administrator shall prepare phased work reports, informing the People's Court of the work done in connection with the takeover.

Article 47 Criteria for takeover

Whether the administrator has taken over the debtor's assets, seals, account books, documents and other materials shall be decided on actual possession or control thereof. In case of actual possession or control by the administrator, the administrator shall be deemed to have taken over of the same. In case of partial possession or control in practice, it shall be deemed as a partial takeover by the administrator.

Chapter II Enterprise Liquidation

Section 4 Investigation of the Assets of the Debtor

Article 48 Scope of the debtor's assets subject to investigation

After accepting the appointment by the People's Court, the administrator shall investigate the assets of the debtor. The scope of the investigation generally includes.

(i) The capital contribution of the debtor's shareholders, which includes: the register of contributors, contribution agreements, articles of association, capital verification reports and actual capital contributions, evaluation reports and approval documents of non-monetary property contributions, property ownership certificates, ownership change registration documents, previous capital changes and the relevant capital verification reports;

(ii) The debtor's monetary assets: cash on hand, bank deposits and other monetary funds;

(iii) The debtor's claims, including: why and when the claims owed to the debtor come into existence, particulars of the claims, actual situation of the debtor's debtors, the collection of claims, whether the claims are involved in actions or arbitration, whether the limitation of action has expired, the time limit for implementing the claims that have been adjudicated in actions or arbitration;

(iv) The debtor's inventory, including its storage location, quantity, status, nature and relevant vouchers;

(v) The debtor's equipment, including their ownership and its duty-free equipment;

(vi) The debtor's vehicles of transport, including the type, quantity, model and condition thereof;

(vii) The debtor's immovables, including land use right, housing ownership, construction in progress, approval documents for unregistered real estate projects, relevant permits, project progress, construction status and relevant technical data;

(viii) The debtor's external investment, including all kinds of investment securities, wholly-owned enterprises, shareholding enterprises and other assets;

(ix) The assets of the debtor's branches, including the assets of the branches and factories having no separate legal personality, offices and other branches;

(x) The debtor's intangible assets, including patent right, trademark right, copyright, license or franchise;

(xi) The business affairs of the debtor;

(xii) Assets of the debtor that can be recovered legally;

(xiii) Executory contracts between the debtor and any other party;

(xiv) Whether the debtor is eligible for tax rebate, refund or any other relief; and

(xv) Other assets and interests in the assets of the debtor that have disposal value.

Article 49 Methods to investigate the debtor's assets

The administrator shall timely investigate the assets of the debtor and its branches. The methods of investigation include: (a) conducting field visits, (b) inquiring of institutions like banks, industrial and commercial administrations, land and resources administrations, real estate authorities, departments of motor vehicles and securities registration authorities, (c) acquiring information from creditors, employees and shareholders and other relevant persons, (d) searching and checking the relevant information online, and (e) applying to the People's Court accepting the bankruptcy case for searching the debtor's asset information via the online enforcement enquiry and control system.

Methods used by the administrator to investigate the debtor's assets generally include:

(i) To investigate the operation status of the debtor. The administrator shall visit the debtor's domicile to investigate its operation status. If the location of the debtor is unknown, the administrator may obtain useful information by visiting the relevant places and taking pictures. In addition, he may retrieve the debtor's industrial and commercial archives from the market supervision and regulation authorities which the debtor registered with, and examine the debtor's registration information and operation status.

(ii) To investigate the assets of the debtor:

A. The administrator may check the cash on hand and all types of documents based on the information, documents and other materials taken over from the debtor. In case of any discrepancy between the accounts and vouchers, the administrator shall require the debtor to provide written explanations and truthfully record the same.

B. For bank deposits, the administrator may, based on the information about the bank accounts already taken over, as well as the information retrieved from the "provincial/local" and "nationwide" enquiry and control system of the court, seek such accounts' basic information, historical transaction records, judicial freezing status, balances and among others, at the account opening banks. Balances on such accounts, if any, shall be promptly transferred to the administrator's account.

The administrator may inquire into whether the debtor has any account on third-party payment and settlement platforms such as Alipay and WeChat Pay, and whether it has any insurance asset or fund under wealth management. If the administrator is unable to take over such assets, he may apply to the Court for inquiring about the debtor's bank account, insurance, wealth management, and accounts on Alipay, WeChat Pay and other third-party payment and settlement platforms, and transferring the balances on such accounts to the administrator's account.

C. With respect to physical assets,

(a) The administrator may check the quantity, state, nature and relevant vouchers of the inventory at the location of its storage. Where the inventory includes any real estate developed by the debtor, the administrator shall verify the filing information regarding the electronically signed contract concerning the pre-sale real estate on the websites of the local real property transaction authorities, and examine the actual possession of the real estate and relevant invoices and vouchers.

(b) The administrator may conduct field investigation and verify the ownership, relevant contracts, certificates and construction documents of the above-ground attachments other than equipment, structures and buildings, and also check the condition of the debtor's custom duty-free equipment;

(c) With respect to the title to real estate, the administrator may obtain relevant registration information from the local real estate registration authorities; the administrator may apply to the state-owned assets management authorities for information retrieval, if the real estate involves state-owned enterprises;

(d) With regards to the title to movables, the administrator may inquire about the vehicles registered under the debtor's name at the department of motor vehicles, and then verify the pertinent titles, vehicle licenses, purchase invoices, insurance policies, car keys and other relevant information;

(e) The administrator may, during the takeover process, inquire into the project approval documents, relevant permits, construction contracts, project and payment progress, construction status and other relevant data presented by the debtor, and take over the relevant materials to check the information of the projects under construction, as the case may be.

D. The administrator may inquire into negotiable securities at securities registration and clearing institutions.

E. The administrator shall thoroughly inquire about the debtor's intangible assets, pursuant to the documents proving the patent, trademark, copyright, domain name, license, franchise or other rights, relevant contracts, term of titles and account records that have been taken over from the debtor; the administrator may also inquire the same on public platforms like China National Intellectual Property Administration.

Chapter II   Enterprise Liquidation

(iii) To investigate the claims of the debtor. The administrator may inquire into matters including: (a) why and when the claims owed to the debtor come into existence, (b) particulars of the claims, (c) information related to the debtor's debtors, (d) collection of claims, (e) whether the claims are involved in actions or arbitration, (f) whether the limitation of action has expired, (g) the time limit for implementing the claims that have been adjudicated in actions or arbitration, and (h) whether the application implementation period has expired. If the administrator verifies the claims by checking the accounts, he shall find out whether the claims are consistent with the accounts, reclassify and record the claims verified, and then confirm thereof.

(iv) To investigate the capital contribution of the debtor's shareholders. The administrator may consult the register of contributors, contribution agreements, articles of association, contribution certificates, capital verification reports and actual capital contributions, documents approving non-monetary property contributions, property ownership certificates, ownership change registration documents, previous capital changes and the relevant capital verification reports. In the absence of capital verification reports, contribution certificates and other materials, the contribution may be determined by the administrator through checking account transaction flows and financial vouchers.

(v) To investigate the debtor's external investment. The administrator may, upon verification of all the relevant data, record the debtor's investment securities, the circumstances of its wholly-owned enterprises and shareholding enterprises, the amount invested, the existing par values of its investment, and the amounts indicated on contribution certificates. With regards to other long-term investments, the administrator may verify the invested subjects, the amount invested, relevant contracts, bills and other documents, and register them after confirmation. Where the debtor is a state-owned enterprise, the administrator may also consult the state-owned assets management authorities about the specific contribution.

(vi) To investigate the possession of the debtor's assets by a third party. The administrator may find out the reasons and grounds for the possession of the assets of the debtor by other parties.

(vii) To investigate the debtor's possession of any assets owned by a third party. The administrator may find out the reasons and grounds for the debtor's possession of any asset owned by a third party, as well as the number of such assets.

(viii) To investigate whether the debtor has any act as stipulated in Article 16, 31, 32 or 33 of the Enterprise Bankruptcy Law.

(ix) To investigate whether any director, supervisor or executive of the debtor has gained abnormal incomes or misappropriated the assets of the debtor by abusing their powers.

(x) To investigate the executory contracts of the debtor.

(xi) To investigate the pending litigation and arbitration involving the debtor, as well as the cases where the judgments have not been fully implemented.

(xii) To investigate whether the debtor has any refundable tax credit. The administrator may enquire from the competent taxing authority whether the debtor has any refundable tax credit. If so, the administrator shall timely apply for tax refund.

(xiii) To investigate other circumstances relating to the debtor's assets.

Article 50 Preparing a report on the assets of the debtor

After investigating the assets of the debtor, the administrator shall prepare a report on the status of such assets based on the information acquired, and timely submit it to the People's Court, the creditors' meeting and the creditors' committee, which may use the report as a reference to decide on relevant matters. Such a report shall contain the basic information of each asset, including its name, specification, model, quantity, ownership status, current situation and book value, etc.

Article 51 Hiring professional firms to perform required audit, evaluation and appraisal work

The administrator may, upon the consent of the People's Court, hire eligible professional firms to, as he deems necessary, audit, evaluate and appraise the debtor's assets by means of organizing public bidding, inviting to bid, asking for a quote or requesting the court to select the firms for him using the rolling-ball lottery method, etc.

Where the financial books taken over by the administrator are incomplete, or with crucial financial information missing, rendering the books obviously unsatisfying the audit requirements, the administrator may report his decision not to have the books audited to the People's Court and the creditors' meeting.

With regards to the cases where the debtor has no assets or its assets are insufficient to pay the bankruptcy expenses, the administrator shall notify the debtor's shareholders, together with any other persons obligated to assist in the liquidation, to pay the audit fees in advance. If the relevant persons fail to do so, the administrator may decide against entrusting the auditing work to a professional firm. If the administrator decides so, he shall notify the known creditors within three days. Where the creditors request the administrator to have the audit done, they shall pay the audit fees in advance.

The debtor may, within six months before applying for bankruptcy liquidation, entrust the auditing to any audit and appraisal firm. Where the administrator decides, upon examination and review, that the audit report and the appraisal report presented conform with the requirements of auditing for bankruptcy and liquidation purposes, the administrator may, after these reports are passed at the creditors' meeting through voting, directly use the conclusions in these reports, and not to otherwise entrust the audit and appraisal work.

Article 52 Compelling the debtor to assist in assets investigation

Where the administrator deems it necessary, he may request the relevant persons of the debtor to assist in his investigation of the debtor's assets. When inquiring into such persons, the administrator shall have two investigators present and keep records, which shall be signed by the two parties upon confirmation.

When the relevant persons of the debtor refuse to assist, the administrator may report in writing to the People's Court, requesting the Court to take corresponding measures to order the former to do so.

Article 53 Statement of circumstances where the assets cannot be fully investigated

In the event of the administrator's failure to thoroughly investigate the assets of the debtor, he may explain the situation in the report on the assets of the debtor.

Section 5 Managing the Internal Affairs of the Debtor

Article 54 Handling of internal management affairs of the debtor before the takeover

Before the takeover of the debtor's assets, seals, account books, documents and other materials, the administrator has the right to require the debtor and its relevant persons to timely report its internal management affairs.

Article 55 Handling of internal management affairs of the debtor after the takeover

The internal management affairs of the debtor shall be, when an administrator has been appointed by the People's Court, decided by the administrator.

Article 56 Developing the rules for managing the internal affairs of the debtor

In order to effectively regulate the management of the debtor's internal affairs, the administrator may formulate rules for managing the debtor's internal affairs and report such rules to the People's Court in writing.

In order to effectively regulate the debtor's overheads and other necessary expenses, the administrator may formulate the debtor's payment rules and communicate such rules to the relevant persons for compliance and implementation, which shall be recorded and filed.

Chapter II Enterprise Liquidation

Article 57 Devising a financial management system

The administrator shall, upon receipt of the People's Court decision to appoint him as the administrator, timely devise a financial management system and report it to the Court. Such a system includes: (a) procedures for opening, using and closing bank accounts; (b) management of the collection and payment of monetary funds; (c) the process for accepting, storing and disposing of assets such as inventory, fixed assets and intangible assets; (d) the process of account composition and write-off; and (e) the rules relating to the powers and process for approving bankruptcy expenses such as travel expenses, clerical costs and agency fees. The system is designed to regulate the financial work of the debtor, including the custody, disposal and distribution of the debtor's assets and the disbursement of bankruptcy expenses.

Article 58 Creating financial positions

The administrator shall, pursuant to the principle of separation of incompatible positions, set up the positions of cashier and accountant.

The cashier is mainly responsible for collection and payment of bank deposits and preparation of journal entries. The accountant is primarily responsible for daily accounting activities, producing financial statements and tax returns, issuing and reviewing invoices, keeping accounting files, and etc.

Article 59 The administrator's decision to continue or cease the debtor's business

Where the administrator, prior to the first creditors' meeting, decides to continue or cease the business of the debtor, he shall report to the People's Court the actual operational circumstances of the debtor, his decision to continue or cease its business and the reasons thereof. Such a decision shall also be approved by the Court.

The administrator may, after the convening of the first creditors' meeting, make a proposal on the continuation or termination of the debtor's business and report the proposal and the pertinent reasons to the creditors' meeting, which shall decide to continue or cease the debtor's business. If the administrator proposes to continue the debtor's business, he may also draft a plan for the management of the debtor's business affairs and report it to the creditors' meeting for deliberation and determination.

Article 60 Criteria for continuation or termination of business

The administrator may determine whether the debtor shall continue or cease its business according to the following criteria.

(i) The debtor shall continue its business if doing so is conducive to appreciating the debtor's assets and raising the percentage of claims being repaid;

(ii) The debtor shall cease its business if doing so is conducive to appreciating the debtor's assets and raising the percentage of claims being repaid.

Chapter II Enterprise Liquidation

Section 6 Management of the Debtor's Assets

Article 61 The administrator's duty to prudently manage and dispose of the debtor's assets

The administrator shall have the duty to prudently manage and dispose of the assets taken over from the debtor according to law.

Article 62 Developing the debtor's asset management plan

The administrator shall formulate the debtor's asset management plan. Generally, such a management plan primarily includes.

(i) Management and maintenance of the debtor's assets, and the budgeting thereof;

(ii) An operation plan for continuing the debtor's business and the budgeting thereof; and

(iii) Scheduling and budgeting for collection of the debtor's assets.

Article 63 Voting on and approval of the asset management plan

The asset management plan drawn up by the administrator shall be submitted to the creditors' meeting for a vote. The administrator shall implement the plan adopted at the creditors' meeting through voting. Where the plan fails to be adopted at the creditors' meeting, the administrator may apply to the People's Court for approval, and carry out the plan upon approval of the Court.

Article 64 Implementation of the asset management plan

With regards to the items whose implementation requires the consent of the creditors' meeting according to law, the administrator is not required to regain the consent of the creditors' meeting when implementing such items, if specific provisions thereon can be found in the asset management plan adopted at the creditors' meeting.

With regards to the items whose implementation requires the approval of the People's Court according to law, the administrator is not required to regain the approval of the Court when implementing such items, if specific provisions thereon can be found in the asset management plan approved by the Court.

Article 65 Supervision over the management and disposition of the debtor's assets

If the administrator finds that the relevant persons of the debtor, upon the People's Court decision to accept the bankruptcy application, have mismanaged and improperly disposed of the debtor's assets, causing damages thereto, the administrator shall have the right to stop and correct such acts according to law, and report the same to the court, creditors' meeting or creditors' committee.

Article 66 Management and disposal measures after takeover

After taking over the debtor's assets, the administrator shall take reasonable measures to manage and dispose of the same, taking into account their different natures. Such measures generally include:

(i) Where the ownership of the debtor's assets is in dispute or pending, the administrator shall claim the relevant rights according to law;

(ii) Where any of the debtor's assets is left idle but ideal for external lease, the administrator may lease it upon the approval of the People's Court or the consent of the creditors' meeting, provided that the lease term is determined on the principle of maximizing the value of the asset in future sales;

(iii) Where any of the debtor's assets is liable to be lost or vulnerable to potential safety hazards, the administrator shall designate special persons to take charge and keep it safe;

(iv) If any of the debtor's assets is fragile, perishable, obviously diminishing value, unsuitable for safekeeping or incurring high safekeeping cost, the administrator shall promptly report to the Court and sell off or dispose of it according to law;

(v) The administrator shall designate special persons to take custody of the debtor's cash, bank deposit certificates and negotiable securities, strictly in accordance with the financial management system;

(vi) In respect of the assets acquired by the debtor through external investment, the administrator shall timely notify the invested enterprises in writing, and legally exercise contributor rights like the rights to assessing to information, receiving dividends, participating in decision-making and voting. In case of the emergence of causes of dissolution, liquidation or bankruptcy of any invested enterprise, the administrator shall perform the duties of shareholders on behalf of the debtor, and deal with the affairs in relation to the dissolution, liquidation or bankruptcy of the invested enterprise;

(vii) The administrator shall timely register or exercise the rights to the debtor's assets in accordance with law, if failing to so may result in the forfeiture of such rights;

(viii) The administrator shall go through the necessary procedures to have the debtor's assets insured, if such assets need to be insured.

Article 67 The administrator's major conduct reporting system

The administrator shall timely report to the Court if he, prior to the first creditors' meeting, commits any of the following acts:

(i) Transferring interests in land, housing or any other immovable;

(ii) Transferring property rights such as mineral exploration right, mining right and intellectual property right;

(iii) Transferring all inventories or business operations;

(iv) Taking out loans;

(v) Providing property as security;

(vi) Transferring claims and negotiable securities;

(vii) Performing the executory contracts between the debtor and any other party;

(viii) Waiving certain rights;

(ix) Recovering the collateral; and

(x) Other disposition of assets that significantly affects the interests of the debtor.

After the first creditors' meeting, if the administrator commits any of the acts prescribed in the preceding paragraph, he shall work out an asset management or realization plan in advance and submit it to a creditors' meeting for voting. If it fails to be adopted at the creditors' meeting, the administrator may not dispose of the assets in question.

The administrator shall, in accordance with Article 69 of the Enterprise Bankruptcy Law, report in writing to the creditors' committee or the People's Court ten days prior to the disposition of any asset. The creditors' committee may, pursuant to the Enterprise Bankruptcy Law, Article 68, Paragraph 2, require the administrator to explain such dispositions or provide the relevant supporting documentation.

The creditors' committee shall have the right to request the administrator to make corrections, if the disposition made by the administrator is considered inconsistent with the asset management or realization plan adopted at a creditors' meeting. If the administrator refuses to rectify, the creditors' committee may request the People's Court to make a decision.

Where the Court holds that any disposition carried out by the administrator fails to conform to the asset management or realization plan adopted at the creditors' meeting, the administrator shall make corrections or carry out the disposition after being reapproved at a creditors' meeting.

Article 68 Submission of executory contracts

Regardless of whether the administrator has taken over the debtor's assets and business affairs, he shall require the debtor to timely submit all the executory contracts signed with any other party before the People's Court's acceptance of the bankruptcy application.

Article 69 Handling of executory contracts

After the People's Court decides to accept the bankruptcy application, the administrator has the right to terminate or continue the performance of any executory contracts signed therebefore, provided that he shall notify any other contracting party and give the reasons behind his decision.

Chapter II Enterprise Liquidation

If the administrator fails to notify the other contracting party within two months from the acceptance date of the bankruptcy application, or fails to reply within thirty days from the receipt date of the relevant notice issued by the other party, the contract concerned shall be deemed terminated.

If the administrator decides to continue the performance of a contract, the other party shall fulfill the contract, provided that the latter has the right to request the provision of security. If the administrator fails to do so, the contract shall be deemed terminated.

Article 70 System for reporting the administrator's decision to continue the performance of contracts

If the administrator, prior to the first creditors' meeting, deems it necessary to continue the performance of any executory contract between the debtor and any other party, he shall report to the People's Court and then decide to continue to perform or terminate the contract in line with the opinions of the Court.

If the administrator, after the first creditors' meeting, deems it necessary to continue the performance of any executory contract between the debtor and any other party, he may decide to continue the performance of the contract and report to the creditors' committee in time. In the absence of a creditors' committee, the administrator shall promptly report to the People's Court.

If the administrator decides to continue the performance of a contract, he shall timely notify the other contracting party. Where the other party requests the administrator to provide security, the administrator shall offer the debtor's assets as security. The contract shall be deemed terminated, if the administrator fails to provide such security or the other party does not accept the security offered.

Article 71 Grounds for the decision to terminate or continue to perform a contract

The administrator shall decide to continue to perform or terminate the contract by considering if an act is conducive to appreciating the debtor's assets and raising the percentage of creditors' claims being repaid;

Article 72 Matters following the termination of a contract

The other contracting party may file a claim against the debtor for damages arising from the termination of a contract between the two parties. The administrator shall require the other party to pay off its debts to the debtor arising from the termination of the contract, if any.

Article 73 Repayment of debts or delivery of assets by the persons owing debts to the debtor or holding its assets

After the People's Court accepts the bankruptcy application, the administrator shall request the persons owing debts to the debtor or holding its assets to pay off their debts or deliver the relevant assets to the administrator.

Where any person owing debts to the debtor or holding its assets intentionally pays off his debts or delivers the assets to the debtor in violation of the provisions of the preceding paragraph, to the detriment of the debtor's creditors, such persons shall not be released from the obligation to repay the debts or deliver the assets, and the administrator shall have the right to require such persons to repay their debts again, redeliver the assets or compensate for the losses arising therefrom.

Article 74 Written notices on repayment of debts or delivery of assets

The administrator shall notify, in writing, persons owing debts to the debtor or holding its assets to timely pay off their debts or deliver the assets to the administrator.

Such a notice shall articulate the following matters, including: (a) time of the Court's acceptance of the bankruptcy application; (b) notices and announcements issued by the People's Court requiring repayment of debts and delivery of assets to the administrator; (c) the amount of debt due by any person to the debtor; (d) names, specifications, quantities and conditions of the assets deliverable by any holder of the debtor's assets; (e) when and how the debts shall be repaid and assets delivered, and (f) legal liability for failure to pay off the debts or deliver the assets.

Chapter II Enterprise Liquidation

Where any person owing debt to the debtor refuses to pay off his debts or any holder of the debtor's assets refuses to deliver the assets, the administrator shall be entitled to bring a lawsuit before the People's Court on behalf of the debtor.

Article 75 The administrator's right of revocation

Where the administrator finds that any of the debtor's assets falls under the circumstances provided in Article 31 or Article 32 of the Enterprise Bankruptcy Law, he shall notify, in writing, the party benefiting from the act to return the assets and any illegitimate benefits, release the security interests or return the secured assets and discharge the debts. If the party refuses to return the same after being notified, the administrator shall promptly file a lawsuit in accordance with Article 9 of the Provisions of the Supreme People's Court on Several Issues Concerning the Application of the Enterprise Bankruptcy Law (II).

Article 76 Liability for compensation bearable by the relevant responsible persons of the debtor

Where the debtor is found to have committed any acts under Article 31 or Article 32, Enterprise Bankruptcy Law, to the detriment of creditors, the administrator is entitled to bring a lawsuit before the People's Court, requesting the Court to order that the persons committing intentional or gross negligence, including the debtor's legal representative and any other directly responsible individual, compensate against the losses suffered by creditors in accordance with the law.

Article 77 The debtor's invalid acts and liability for compensation

Where the debtor is found to have committed any act prescribed in Article 33 of the Enterprise Bankruptcy Law, the administrator is entitled to demand the return of the assets from the party who has acquired the same as a result of such act. If the party refuses to do so, the administrator has the right to bring a lawsuit before the People's Court, requesting the Court to declare the invalidity of that party's acquisition of the assets from the debtor.

Where the debtor has committed any acts under the Enterprise Bankruptcy Law, Article 33, to the detriment of creditors, the administrator is entitled to bring a lawsuit before the Court, requesting the Court to order that the debtor's legal representative, as well as any other directly responsible individual, compensate against the losses suffered by creditors in accordance with the law.

Article 78 Call for unfunded capital commitment

Where any capital contributor of the debtor is found to have not fully fulfilled his capital commitment, the administrator shall request the contributor to pay for the unfunded capital commitment, without being subject to the time limit for contribution. If such a contributor refuses to do so, the administrator shall bring a lawsuit before the People's Court, requesting the Court to order the contributor to pay.

If the administrator decides to waive the right to bring a lawsuit, he shall first solicit opinions from the creditors' meeting.

Article 79 Call for surreptitiously withdrawn capital contributions

Where any contributor of the debtor is found to have surreptitiously withdrawn his capital contribution, the administrator shall require the contributor to return such capital. In the event that such a contributor refuses to do so, the administrator has the right to bring a lawsuit before the People's Court, demanding the recovery thereof.

With regards to any director and/or senior executive responsible for supervising shareholders' performance of their capital contribution obligations, or any other shareholder, director, senior executive and/or actual controller who has assisted the shareholder in the surreptitious withdrawal of his capital contribution, the administrator is entitled to require that such persons be jointly and severally liable for all the harms caused by the shareholder's default of his obligation of capital contribution or by his surreptitious withdrawal of capital contribution.

Where the administrator, in the bankruptcy proceedings, decides to waive the recovery of such withdrawn capital, opinions of the creditors' meeting shall be solicited first.

Chapter II Enterprise Liquidation

Article 80 Liability of the debtor's senior executives to return assets or compensate for losses

Where any director, supervisor and senior executive of the debtor is found to have gained abnormal incomes or misappropriated the assets of the debtor by abusing their powers, the administrator shall recover the same or require such persons to compensate for the losses incurred thereby. If such persons refuse to return the assets or compensate for the losses, the administrator has the right to bring a lawsuit against them before the People's Court, demanding the return or compensation. In cases where a crime is suspected, the cases may be referred to the public security authorities to investigate for criminal responsibility.

Article 81 The administrator's recovery of pledged collateral and assets encumbered with liens

After taking over the debtor's assets, the administrator may, with the purpose to appreciate the debtor's assets and raise the percentage of creditors' claims being repaid, recover the pledged collateral or assets encumbered with liens, by redeeming the relevant debts or providing alternative security acceptable to creditors.

Where the administrator, for the purpose of recovering the pledged collateral or assets encumbered with liens, discharges the relevant debts or provides alternative security acceptable to the creditor, the market values of such assets at the time of pledge or encumbrance shall be used as references, if the value of such an asset is lower than the amount of the secured claim.

Article 82 System for reporting the recovery of pledged collateral and assets encumbered with liens

If the administrator, prior to the convening of the first creditors' meeting, deems it necessary to recover the pledged collateral or assets encumbered with liens by discharging the relevant debts or providing alternative security acceptable to the creditors, the administrator shall obtain the prior consent of the People's Court.

If the administrator, after the convening of the first creditors' meeting, deems it necessary to recover the pledged collateral or assets encumbered with liens, he may recover the same by discharging the relevant debts or offering alternative security acceptable to the creditors. The administrator shall draw up an asset management or realization plan in advance and submit it to a vote at the creditors' meeting. If the plan fails to be adopted at the creditors' meeting, and also fails to be approved by the Court in accordance with Article 65 of the Enterprise Bankruptcy Law, the administrator shall not dispose of the assets in question.

The administrator shall report in writing to the creditors' committee ten days preceding the disposition of any asset. In the absence of a creditors' committee, a written report shall be submitted to the Court ten days prior to any disposition.

Article 83 An Obligees' recovery of assets from the debtor

In the process where the administrator takes over the debtor's assets, an obligee may claim to recover the assets not owned by, but in the possession of the debtor, by virtue of the Enterprise Bankruptcy Law, Article 38. The administrator shall return the assets to the obligee if the latter's claims are authenticated.

In cases where the obligee's claims are disallowed by the administrator, he may inform the obligee to file a lawsuit before the People's Court which has accepted the bankruptcy case, requesting to exercise his right of recovery. However, the takeover shall not be suspended during the litigation period.

Where an asset claimed by the obligee is in the legal possession of the debtor, the administrator shall have the right to demand the obligee to redeem any debt that may arise from his recovery of the asset.

Article 84 Examination of the obligee's claims for relief

Where any asset recoverable by an obligee is lost, or damaged prior to the Court's acceptance of the bankruptcy application, the obligee may make claims with respect to such loss or damages.

Chapter II Enterprise Liquidation

Where a third party is liable for the loss of or damages to any asset recoverable by the obligee preceding the Court's acceptance of the bankruptcy application, or an insurer is liable to pay compensation therefor, the obligee's right of recovery is directly offset by compensation.

If any asset recoverable by an obligee is lost, or damaged due to the performance of duties by the administrator or any relevant person after the People's Court's acceptance of the bankruptcy application, the debt arising therefrom shall be considered a debt incurred in the common interests of creditors. The obligee may make a claim against the administrator to discharge the debt with the debtor's assets.

Article 85 Review of a request for restoring a subject matter in transit

There are cases where the seller has already shipped the subject-matter of a sale to the debtor (i.e., the buyer) when the People's Court accepts the bankruptcy application, but the debtor has neither received the shipment nor paid full price. If the seller claims to take back the subject matter under this circumstance, the administrator shall decide whether to approve or reject such claims by considering if doing so will help appreciate the debtor's assets and raise the percentage of creditors' claims being repaid.

If the administrator agrees to the seller's request of reclamation, he shall notify the seller in writing.

Where the administrator refuses the seller's request, he shall pay the full purchase price with the debtor's assets and notify the seller in writing to deliver the subject matter.

Article 86 Right of offset

Any creditor who also owes debts to the debtor prior to the Court's acceptance of the bankruptcy application shall have the right to request for setoff. If such requests are believed to satisfy the following requirements upon examination by the administrator, the administrator may notify such creditors, in writing, to confirm the setoff, which shall take effect from the receipt date of the notice by the administrator:

(i) The absence of any of the three circumstances provided in Article 40, Enterprise Bankruptcy Law;

(ii) The claims have been filed according to law and authenticated, unanimously and beyond any reasonable doubt, by a creditors' meeting;

(iii) There is no dispute over the mutual credits/debts between the creditor and the debtor, or such a relationship has been confirmed by effective legal documents;

(iv) The claims whose limitation of actions or period of compulsory enforcement has not expired;

(v) The request for setoff is made before the final distribution of assets in bankruptcy;

(vi) The request does not involve any debts that may not be set off according to law. "Any debts that may not be set off according to law" include: the claims enjoyed by a shareholder of the debtor shall not be set off against his unpaid capital commitment to the debtor; such shareholder's claims shall not be set off against his debt to the debtor arising out of his surreptitious withdrawal of capital contribution; and subordiniated claims may not be set off against the debts due to the debtor.

If the administrator disagrees with a claim for setoff, he shall file a lawsuit with the People's Court within the agreed period of objection or three months following the receipt date of the notice of the claim for setoff.

Where the People's Court dismisses the administrator's request for invalidating the setoff, such setoff shall take effect from the date when the administrator receives the notice of the claim for setoff.

The administrator may not proactively set off the mutual debts between the debtor and the creditor, except for the circumstances where such setoff benefits the assets of the debtor.

Article 87 Recourse to assets

After obtaining the clues to the relevant assets, the administrator shall first fully investigate and then recover the assets through means like negotiation and litigation. Where it is necessary to suspend the recovery of the assets or to waive the right of recourse, he shall do so only after a thorough review and analysis, and having the consent of the creditors' meeting.

Section 7 Registration and Inspection of Claims

Article 88 Receiving the documents for filing a claim

The administrator shall receive the documents provided by the creditors for filing claims within the time limit and at the place as announced by the People's Court for lodging claims.

When receiving claim filing at the designated place, the administrator may have some documents in place, including Instructions for Lodging a Claim, Claim Form, Confirmation of Creditors' Address and Contact Information, and Checklist of Documents for Filing a Claim, etc.

The administrator shall, upon receiving a claimant's claims and supporting documentation, issue a receipt to the claimant.

The administrator shall enquire in writing about the debtor's payment of taxes, social insurance contributions, housing provident funds and other payables, and notify the competent authorities to file their claims.

Article 89 Documents required for filing of a claim

When receiving the documents provided by creditors for lodging claims, the administrator shall require:

(i) Where a creditor files a claim on his own, a valid form of identification shall be presented if the creditor is a natural person; in the case of a legal person or a non-legal-person entity, the required documents include: the business license for legal person, or any other qualification certificate of a legal person or a non-legal-person entity, together with the valid identification of the legal representative or the person in charge;

(ii) If a creditor files a claim through an agent, the agent shall provide both the power of attorney signed and stamped by the principal and his own identification. Where the agent is a lawyer, he shall also provide the appointment letter issued by his law firm and his lawyer's practice certificate. If the agent attends a creditors' meeting and votes at such meetings, a special power of attorney shall also be presented;

(iii) A creditor shall, as required by the administrator, truthfully complete the Claim Form, Confirmation of Creditors' Address and Contact Information, and other documents listed in Article 88 hereof, specifying the amount claimed, whether there is any security on property and how the claim came into being. The creditor shall also provide relevant supporting documentation.

Article 90 Registration of documents provided for filing claims

The administrator shall, following receipt of the documents submitted by claimants for filing claims, register the same and maintain a Register of Claims on the basis thereof. The claims filed, no matter whether they can be accepted as bankruptcy claims or not, shall be recorded in such a book.

The Register of Claims generally contains the following information:

(i) Basic information of a creditor: name of the creditor (enterprise or individual), position and address of the legal representative or person in charge of the enterprise, the creditor's bank and contact information; in case of an agent being entrusted, the name, address, contact details and authority of the agent shall also be specified;

(ii) Basic information of a claim: particulars of why the claim came into being, proof of the claim, maturity date of the claim, filing time, the amount of debt claimed (including the original debt and all accrued but unpaid interest on the debt), and particulars of whether it is a secured claim, whether there are contingent on conditions and time limits, whether it is a joint claim, whether there is any joint debtor, and whether it is based on a right of recourse or future right of recourse; and

(iii) Other matters that are considered necessary by the administrator.

Article 91 *Pro forma* review of the claims filed

When conducting pro forma review of the documents produced by a creditor to file a claim, the administrator primarily inspects the creditor's identification, whether the obligor is the debtor in the bankruptcy case, and the category and nature of the claim. If the claimant is found to dissatisfy the requirements upon the pro forma review, the administrator shall notify the claimant in writing to provide the missing documents within a reasonable time limit. The claimant shall be also informed of the consequences in case he fails to do so, or in cases where the documents remain unacceptable even after he has done so. Under this circumstance, the administrator may reject the claim, and issue a letter of refusing to accept as required by the claimant.

Chapter II Enterprise Liquidation

Article 92 Substantial review of the claims filed

The administrator shall conduct substantial review of the claims filed, including their authenticity, legality and timeliness. When inspecting documents provided by a creditor to file a claim, the administrator shall generally pay attention to the following issues:

(i) In the event any interest, penalty interest, liquidated damages and/or late fee have generated on the debt claimed by a creditor, such amounts shall cease to accrue after the acceptance of the bankruptcy application.

(ii) Fines and penalties imposed by administrative or judicial authorities on the debtor do not fall under the category of general claims.

(iii) An undue debt claimed shall be considered due when the bankruptcy case is accepted.

(iv) With respect to conditional claims against the debtor, the administrator shall examine whether the conditions attached have been fulfilled; in case of unfulfillment, the determination of such claims shall be deferred.

(v) The determination of claims involved in pending actions or arbitrations shall be deferred.

(vi) Joint creditors may choose one among them to file their claims on their behalf, or file them jointly. A claim filed in this circumstance shall be considered one debt against the debtor.

(vii) In the case a creditor fails to submit all his claims to the administrator, and the debtor's guarantor or any other joint debtor has not paid off the debts on behalf of the debtor, but the creditor files claim by virtue of his future right of recourse to the debtor, the administrator shall register such claims but defer the determination thereof.

(viii) Where a creditor fails to timely make his claims against the debtor, but he later submits his claims to the administrator in accordance with Article 536 of the Civil Code of the PRC, the administrator shall register and inspect such claims.

(ix) Where a creditor files, separately, all his claims against each of the joint debtors in a bankruptcy case, the administrator shall register and inspect such claims. Also, the administrator shall request the creditor to provide truthful written explanations.

(x) Where a creditor files his claims by virtue of his right to compensation for the damages caused by the termination of a contract initiated by the administrator or the debtor pursuant to the Enterprise Bankruptcy Law, the amount of claim shall be determined in line with the actual damages arising therefrom.

(xi) If the entrusted party to an entrustment contract between him and the debtor (i.e., the entrusting party), without knowledge of the debtor's bankruptcy, continues to deal with the entrusted business after the People's Court's acceptance of the bankruptcy application, the administrator shall accept the claims filed by the entrusted party by virtue of his right of claim derived therefrom.

Where the entrusted party continues the entrusted business with knowledge of the debtor's bankruptcy, the administrator shall not accept the claims made thereon, except for the circumstances where the entrusted party shall, as stipulated in the entrustment contract, continue to deal with the entrusted business after the Court's acceptance of the bankruptcy application or otherwise provided by law.

If the entrusted party files claims by virtue of his right of claim derived from his continued dealing of the entrusted business for the benefit of the debtor before the administrator or the debtor asks him to stop doing so, the administrator may discharge the relevant debt as a debt incurred in the common interests of creditors, respective of the entrusted party's knowledge or ignorance of the debtor's bankruptcy, provided that ceasing the entrusted business will prejudice the interests of the debtor.

(xii) Where the debtor is the drawer of a negotiable instrument, and the drawee continues to pay or accept the instrument, the administrator shall register and handle the claims lodged by the drawee according to his right of claim derived therefrom.

(xiii) In the case of any secured claims filed by a creditor, the administrator shall review: (a) legal effects of the security right; (b) the order in which creditors shall be repaid if the asset is secured to two or more creditors; (c) whether the security provided may be revoked according to law; (d) the value of the secured asset; and (e) the extent to which a secured claim is payable. If the value of a secured asset is less than the amount of a secured claim, the amount claimable is subject to the former, and the portion of the claim exceeding such value shall be regarded as a general claim.

Chapter II Enterprise Liquidation

(xiv) Where the proof of a debt submitted by a creditor to the administrator is a legal document with enforceable effect, the administrator may directly confirm the amount of debt specified in such a document, along with the existence or absence of any security on assets. If the debt specified therein is not indicated through the amount of money, the administrator may convert it into the latter in line with its market value. In principle, the conversion date shall be the date on which the People's Court accepts the bankruptcy application.

(xv) Where the claim filed by a creditor with the administrator involves any pending action or arbitration, the administrator may request the People's Court to determine a temporary amount and nature of the claim.

Article 93 Investigation and announcement of employees' claims

The debtor's employees need not file their claims. The administrator shall, after investigation, prepare a list of such claims and have it publicly announced. Such claims include: (a) salaries, healthcare subsidies, disability pensions, and bereavement awards due to the employees; (b) unpaid primary endowment and medical insurance contributions that should have been credited to the employees' personal accounts; and (c) the severance payable to the employees as prescribed by relevant laws and administrative regulations.

The administrator shall investigate the claims of the employees according to the debtor's financial information, personnel archives, attendance records and other documents of proof, and may, when necessary, verify the situation with relevant personnel of the debtor, and request relevant information from competent authorities like the social security authorities and the housing provident fund management authorities.

The time limit and method for announcing the employees' claims, along with the time limit and method for raising objections thereto shall be reasonably determined by considering the number of employees and other actual situations.

If an employee, who has any objection to whatever recorded in the list of the employees' claims, requests the administrator to make corrections, the administrator shall timely review such records and notify the employee of the result in writing. Where the administrator decides not to correct upon review, he shall timely inform the employee of the same with reasonable explanations, and tell the latter that he may file a lawsuit with the People's Court which has accepted the bankruptcy case, requesting a confirmation of his claims.

Article 94 Procedures for inspection of the claims filed

The administrator shall register the documents received from a creditor for filing claims, inspect such claims and prepare a form of claims. In case of a claim with an indefinable nature or the one whose amount is difficult to determine due to its complex structure, the administrator shall contact the creditor, requesting the latter to provide further documentation.

The administrator shall produce Inspection Opinions on a Claim for each claimant, specifying the inspection results, remarks on raising any objection thereto, disallowance of certain claims and reasons therefor, and then notify the creditor in writing. The notice shall indicate that, an objection to the Inspection Opinions, if any, shall be submitted in writing to the administrator within the prescribed period, accompanied by any and all supporting documentation.

If a creditor raises any objection to the Inspection Opinions, the administrator shall review the objection and inform the creditor of the review results. Where the creditor is dissatisfied with the results, the administrator shall tell him that he may file a lawsuit before the Court having accepted the bankruptcy application, or file for arbitration as agreed before the bankruptcy application was accepted.

The administrator shall, according to the results of inspection on the claims, prepare a form of claims and submit it to the creditors' meeting for review. Examples of the inspection results include: the nature and amount of a claim, whether it is a secured or unsecured claim, and whether its statute of limitation or period of compulsory enforcement has expired.

Article 95 Preparation of a form of claims

The administrator shall compile a form of claims in line with the results of inspection.

The administrator shall record all the claims, accepted or disallowed upon inspection, separately into the form of claims. Such a form shall record the claims by their categories determined upon inspection, such as secured claims, unsecured claims, claims with certain conditions or time limits, and claims involving a pending action or arbitration. In addition, the name of the creditor, the amount of the claim, why the claim came into being and the related explanations shall also be indicated under each category. Details of the secured asset shall be added in case of a secured claim.

Article 96 Inspection of, objection to and confirmation of the form of claims

The administrator shall, following completion of the form of claims, timely prepare a report requesting a creditors' meeting to verify the claims, and then submit the report, which must be accompanied by the said form, to the creditors' meeting for review.

If neither the creditor nor the debtor has any objection to the claims recorded in the form of claims, the administrator shall request the People's Court to make a ruling on their confirmation.

Where the debtor or the creditor has any objection to the claims recorded, the administrator shall inform the objector in writing to bring a lawsuit before the People's Court, with respect to the confirmation of claims, within fifteen days upon the verification conducted by a creditors' meeting. If the objector fails to do so, the administrator shall submit a report to the Court, stating the particulars of the objection, the review and the objector's failure to bring a lawsuit, and requesting the Court to make a ruling on confirmation of the claims concerned.

Article 97 Revision of the form of claims

Where errors are found concerning the claims recorded in the form of claims, the administrator shall revise the form and submit the revised form of claims to a creditors' meeting.

The inspection of, objection to and confirmation of the said revised form of claims shall be handled according to Article 96 hereof.

Article 98 Late submission of claims

A creditor, who fails to file his claims within the time limit for filing of claims as specified by the People's Court, may submit his claims to the administrator later but preceding the final distribution of assets in bankruptcy. However, any asset that has already been distributed will not be redistributed to such a creditor. The administrator, after receiving the documents of the late submitted claims, shall register and record the same, and prepare a form of late submitted claims upon inspection. He shall then submit the form to a creditors' meeting for verification. In case of late submitted claims, the administrator has the right to require the creditor concerned to bear the expenses arising out of examining and confirming those claims. Such expenses may include reasonable costs such as the administrator's hourly labor costs, travel expenses and the expenses for convening creditors' meetings.

If a creditor brings a lawsuit before the People's Court without first submitting his claims to the administrator, the administrator shall notify the creditor to timely file his claims and claim his rights in accordance with the procedures for filing bankruptcy claims. Where the creditor files his claims pursuant thereto, the administrator shall timely draw his inspection conclusions.

Article 99 Safekeeping and consulting of the form of claims, register of claims and the documents required for the filing of claims

The form of claims, register of claims and the documents required for the filing of claims shall be kept under the custody of the administrator during the bankruptcy process. Creditors, debtors and other interested parties are entitled to consult these documents.

Section 8　Convening of Creditors' Meetings

Article 100 Convening of the first creditors' meeting

The first creditors' meeting shall be convened by the People's Court. The administrator may recommend the candidates for the chairman of the creditors' meeting to the Court, accompanied by a statement of the basic information about the candidates and the grounds for such recommendation.

Article 101 Preparation for a creditors' meeting

Before the convening of the first creditors' meeting, the administrator shall assist the People's Court in preparing for the meeting and timely submit the necessary documents to the latter.

Article 102 Documents required for the first creditors' meeting

Documents required for the first creditors' meeting mainly include:
(i) Agenda of the meeting;
(ii) Creditor attendance form and minutes signature form;
(iii) Work report of the administrator;
(iv) Inspection report of claims, and form of claims;
(v) Ballots and claim verification forms;
(vi) The debtor's asset management plan;
(vii) A plan for realizing assets in bankruptcy;
(viii) A remuneration scheme for the administrator;
(ix) Particulars about the placement of employees, and payment of salaries, severance and social insurance contributions;
(x) Other matters that should be stated in accordance with the People's Court.

Article 103 Call for the convening of creditors' meetings by the administrator

After the first creditors' meeting, the administrator may call, in line with his work progress and as necessary, for the chairman to convene a creditors' meeting. In that case, he shall provide the chairman with the time, venue and topics of the proposed creditors' meeting.

Under any of the following circumstances, the administrator shall call for the chairman to convene a creditors' meeting to consider the relevant matters:

(i) The form of late submitted claims and revised form of claims should be verified by a creditors' meeting;

(ii) The debtor's asset management plan should be adopted at a creditors' meeting;

(iii) Whether to continue or cease the business operation of the debtor should be decided at a creditors' meeting;

(iv) A reorganization plan should be adopted at a creditors' meeting;

(v) A conciliation agreement should be adopted at a creditors' meeting;

(vi) A plan for realizing assets in bankruptcy should be adopted at a creditors' meeting;

(vii) A plan for distributing assets in bankruptcy should be adopted at a creditors' meeting;

(viii) Other matters, as the People's Court deems necessary, should be decided by a creditors' meeting.

If the chairman of the creditors' meeting refuses to convene the meeting or fails to perform the duties of presiding thereover, the administrator may file with the Court, requesting the convening of a creditors' meeting and the appointment of a new chairman.

Article 104 Notice of a creditors' meeting by the administrator

A creditors' meeting shall be notified by the administrator, irrespective of whether it is called by him. The administrator shall, fifteen days prior to the meeting, notify all creditors of the time, place and topics of the meeting. Documents relating to the exercise of voting rights by creditors shall be sent to creditors in advance. A meeting notice may be delivered in person, or via mail, facsimile or email, in a safe and efficient manner. The administrator shall keep records of all the relevant notices of meetings.

Upon the consent of all known creditors, the People's Court may shorten the said notice period in case of bankruptcies that are processed in an expedited procedure.

Article 105 Ways to convene a creditors' meeting and the voting methods

A creditors' meeting may be convened physically or non-physically, where votes may be cast accordingly.

At a non-physical creditor's meeting, creditors may vote in writing via facsimile, text message, email, instant message, communication group and other means of communication. In that case, the administrator shall inform creditors of the matters to be considered, and the voting procedures and rules in advance; he shall then notify creditors of the voting results by letter, email, announcement or other reasonable means within three days after the convening of the creditors' meeting.

The administrator shall timely retrieve the electronic data recording the voting by means of, among others, printing and photographing, which shall then be stamped by himself or signed off by two staff members. If the voting is conducted at a virtual meeting, the administrator shall keep the relevant audio and video recordings or electronic speech records.

Article 106 The administrator's attendance at creditors' meetings as a nonvoting member

The performance of the administrator's duties shall be subject to the supervision of the creditors' meeting and the creditors' committee.

The administrator shall attend creditors' meetings as a nonvoting member, where he shall report the performance of his duties and answer the inquiries from the meeting members.

If the creditors' meeting or creditors' committee requests the administrator to explain certain affairs within his remit or submit relevant documents, the administrator shall do so accordingly.

Section 9 Representing the Debtor in Actions, Arbitration or Other Legal Proceedings

Article 107 Removal and suspension of protection measures

If the measures to protect the debtor's assets have not been removed or the relevant enforcement procedure has not been suspended after the People's Court accepts the bankruptcy application, the administrator may request the Court or the arbitral body in writing to remove or suspend the same according to law.

Article 108 Suspension of dispute resolution proceedings

After the Court accepts the bankruptcy application, if any pending civil action or arbitration involving the debtor has not been suspended, the administrator may request the Court or the arbitral body in writing to suspend such proceedings according to law.

Article 109 Resumption of legal proceedings

After taking over the assets of the debtor, the administrator may request the People's Court or an arbitration institution to resume any suspended action or arbitration. The administrator shall participate in such actions or arbitration as the debtor's representative.

In cases where the administrator has not taken over the assets of the debtor, or has only taken over the assets in part, the administrator may also request the People's Court or the arbitration institution to resume a suspended action or arbitration involving the debtor, provided that such resumption, in the opinions of the administrator, will not be affected by the takeover.

Article 110 Jurisdiction over lawsuits after the acceptance of bankruptcy cases

After the People's Court accepts the bankruptcy application, any civil action initiated by the administrator involving the debtor may only be brought before the Court that has accepted the bankruptcy application. Where an arbitration clause agreed by the debtor and any third party is applicable to a dispute between the two, such clause shall prevail.

Article 111 Representing the debtor in actions and arbitration

After the Court accepts the bankruptcy application, the administrator shall participate in civil actions and arbitration involving the debtor on behalf of the latter.

During the period of supervision over the implementation of a reorganization plan, the administrator shall represent the debtor in pending actions and arbitration initiated before the start of the supervision period. However, except as otherwise articulated in the reorganization plan, the administrator will not represent the debtor in such actions or arbitration arising from facts or events occurring after the termination of the reorganization procedure.

The administrator may entrust an agent, if he should participate in actions, arbitration or other legal proceedings on behalf of the debtor.

Section 10 Realization of Assets in Bankruptcy

Article 112 Formulating a plan for realizing the assets in bankruptcy

The administrator shall timely draw up a plan for realizing the assets in bankruptcy.

Assets in bankruptcy shall be realized through auction, unless otherwise decided on by the creditors' meeting. The auction announcement shall contain particulars like disclosure of defects, and who bears the tax burden.

Any asset which shall not be auctioned or whose transfer is restricted as provided for by State law, shall be disposed of in a manner as prescribed by the State.

With respect to any asset that may not be realized through auction sales, the administrator may propose in the asset realization plan to realize the same by means of, among others, selling off the asset himself, transferring it by bidding or agreement, hiring an agent to sell it or distribute it in kind at the time of distribution in bankruptcy.

Article 113 Deliberation of the plan for realizing the assets in bankruptcy

The plan prepared by the administrator for realizing the assets in bankruptcy shall be submitted to a creditors' meeting for consideration. It shall be deemed adopted if approved by at least 50% creditors present at the meeting who have voting rights and account for at least 50% of the total unsecured claims. If the plan fails to be adopted at the meeting, the administrator may apply to the People's Court for approval.

Article 114 Sale of assets in bankruptcy

The administrator shall sell off, when and as appropriate, an asset in bankruptcy at reduced price according to the asset realization plan adopted at a creditors' meeting or approved by the People's Court.

If items unsuitable for long-term storage or requiring high custody costs, such as seasonal, fresh, perishable and fragile items, and items losing value quickly, need to be disposed of prior to the first creditors' meeting, the administrator shall dispose of the same timely before the meeting upon approval of the People's Court.

Article 115 Principles for entrusting auctions or selling off by the administrator himself

The administrator shall adhere to the principles of transparency, fairness and impartiality when entrusting an auction or selling off the assets by himself.

Section 11 Distribution of Assets in Bankruptcy

Article 116 Preparing a plan for the distribution of assets in bankruptcy

The administrator shall timely formulate a plan for the distribution of assets in bankruptcy, taking into consideration the real value realized through the sale of such assets. The distribution plan shall specify the following matters:

(i) Names and domiciles of the creditors who will have a share in the distribution of assets in bankruptcy;

(ii) Amount of claims eligible to have a share in the distribution of assets in bankruptcy;

(iii) Amount of assets in bankruptcy available for distribution;

(iv) Order of priority for distributing assets in bankruptcy, and the proportion and amount distributed to different creditors;

(v) Methods for distributing assets in bankruptcy;

(vi) Other matters that should be specified as otherwise stated herein.

Article 117 Ways to pay secured claims

The payment of secured claims against the debtor will not be specified in the plan for the distribution of assets in bankruptcy. The gains realized through the sale of a secured asset shall be employed to prioritize the satisfaction of the claim secured by that asset. If the gains realized therefrom are greater than the amount of the secured claim, the difference shall be listed in the assets in bankruptcy. Where the former is less than the latter, the unsatisfied part of claim may seek its particular share of the general asset distribution as a general claim.

Article 118 Order of priority and principles for repayment

The assets in bankruptcy shall, after the bankruptcy expenses and the debts incurred in the common interests of creditors have got paid first, be liquidated to pay the following in order of priority:

(i) Salaries, healthcare subsidies, disability pensions, and bereavement awards due to the employees; unpaid primary endowment and medical insurance contributions that should have been credited to the employees' personal accounts; and the severance payable to the employees as prescribed by relevant laws and administrative regulations.

(ii) Social insurance contributions (other than those specified in the preceding subparagraph) and taxes unpaid by the debtor;

(iii) General claims; and

(iv) Punitive claims, such as liquidated damages, compensation, fines and penalties, arising prior to the acceptance of the bankruptcy case.

Assets in bankruptcy shall be distributed in cash, except as otherwise decided by a creditors' meeting.

With regards to a claim whose payment priority is not specified in law, the administrator may reasonably determine its payment in adherence to the principle of prioritizing the satisfaction of personal injury claims over property claims, private law claims over public law claims, and compensatory claims over punitive claims.

Article 119　Deliberation of the plan for the distribution of assets in bankruptcy

The plan prepared by the administrator for the distribution of assets in bankruptcy shall be submitted to a creditors' meeting for deliberation. It shall be deemed adopted if approved by at least 50% creditors present at the meeting who have voting rights and account for at least 50% of the total unsecured claims.

Article 120　Second vote on the plan for distribution of assets in bankruptcy

In the event that a plan for distribution of assets in bankruptcy is adopted at a creditors' meeting, the administrator shall lodge it with the People's Court for approval. In case of its failure to be adopted, the administrator shall revise the plan before submitting it to a creditors' meeting for a second vote. If unadopted in the second vote, the administrator may apply to the Court for approval.

Article 121 Implementation of the plan for distribution of assets in bankruptcy

The plan for distribution of assets in bankruptcy, as approved by the People's Court, shall be implemented by the administrator.

Article 122 Announcement of distribution of assets in bankruptcy

Where the assets are distributed multiple times according to the asset distribution plan, the administrator shall announce the amounts of assets distributed and debts discharged each time. Where a final distribution is applicable, the administrator shall state in the announcement the particulars on the delivery or distribution of the amount held in escrow on the announcement date of the final distribution.

Article 123 Termination of bankruptcy proceedings

If the bankrupt has no distributable assets, the administrator shall request the Court to order the termination of the bankruptcy proceedings.

When the final distribution of assets in bankruptcy is completed, the administrator shall timely report to the Court, requesting the termination of the bankruptcy proceedings.

Chapter II Enterprise Liquidation

Section 12 Placing of Certain Assets in Bankruptcy in Escrow and Its Announcement

Article 124 Escrow and announcement

The asset distribution plan prepared by the administrator shall explain the circumstances where certain assets will be placed in escrow.

With respect to a claim involving a pending action or arbitration at the time of asset distribution, the administrator shall place the corresponding share of distribution in escrow. Where the said share of distribution remains uncollected two years after the termination date of the bankruptcy proceedings, the Court shall distribute the asset held in escrow to other creditors.

With respect to a contingent claim whose validity or rescission is dependent upon specific conditions, the administrator shall place the corresponding share of distribution in escrow. The asset held in escrow shall be distributed to other creditors, if the validity conditions are unsatisfied or the rescission conditions are met on the announcement date of the final distribution. Instead, the asset held in escrow shall be handed over to the creditor concerned, if the validity conditions are satisfied or the rescission conditions are not met on the announcement date of the final distribution.

The administrator shall place in escrow a creditor's share of asset distribution uncollected by the latter. Where a creditor fails to collect his share two months after the announcement date of the final distribution, he shall be deemed to have waived his right to distribution, and the administrator shall distribute such shares to other creditors.

Section 13 Termination of the Administrator's Duties

Article 125 The administrator's termination of performance of his duties

In the event that (a) a debtor does not have enough assets to satisfy the bankruptcy costs and the liability incurred in the common interests of creditors, (b) the bankrupt has no distributable assets, or (c) the People's Court orders the termination of the bankruptcy proceedings upon the completion of asset distribution, the administrator shall, within ten days of the Court order of termination of proceedings, bring the order with him to go through the formalities to have the debtor or bankrupt deregistered with its registration authority. On the day after the completion of such deregistration, the administrator shall be discharged from his duties, except those requiring his continued performance.

Article 126 Cancellation of tax registration

The administrator shall, within 10 days after the termination of the bankruptcy liquidation proceedings, go through the formalities to cancel the tax registration for the debtor or the bankrupt.

The cancellation of tax registration requires the submission of the relevant documents as required by the competent taxation bureau at the place where the debtor is domiciled.

Article 127 Proper storage and safekeeping of documents received from the debtor

After ceasing the performance of his duties according to law, the administrator shall hand over the relevant documents taken over from the bankrupt to its superior competent authority or shareholders for safekeeping. In the absence of such authorities or the ignorance of the shareholders' whereabouts, the documents may be sent to an archival institution for safekeeping. The administrator may set aside a certain amount of money from the bankruptcy costs to pay the charges for safekeeping the account books, documents and other archival materials of the debtor or the bankrupt.

Article 128 Closure of bank accounts and destruction of seals

Where the administrator ceases the performance of his duties, he shall, in accordance with relevant regulations, timely go through the procedures of closing his bank account and submitting his seal to the public security authorities for destruction, and report the same to the Court.

Section 14 Special Provisions on the Cases Transferred from Enforcement to Bankruptcy Proceedings and the Summary Proceedings

Article 129 Proceedings applicable to cases transferred from enforcement to bankruptcy proceedings

Where summary proceedings are applied to a case transferred from enforcement to bankruptcy proceedings, the administrator shall complete the processing of the case within three months from the filing date of the "bankruptcy" case, to ensure a timely termination of the proceedings. If any exceptional circumstance calls for an extension of such a time limit, it may be extended by three months upon approval of the Court.

If a case is considered to be too complex to apply the summary proceedings, the administrator shall request the Court to make an order to transfer the case to general proceedings. Matters already decided on under the summary proceedings shall continue to be valid upon the transfer.

Article 130 Reusability of asset information obtained under the enforcement proceedings

The administrator may not reinvestigate the assets ascertained under the enforcement proceedings, such as the debtor's bank deposits, real estate, vehicles, equity, securities and Alipay accounts. However, if the relevant information is obtained more than six months as of the acceptance date of a bankruptcy application, the administrator shall apply for a reinvestigation.

Article 131 Investigation of property rights

The administrator shall investigate the trademark, patent, copyright, domain name and other property rights under the possession of the debtor.

Chapter II Enterprise Liquidation

Where an interested party produces new clues to the debtor's assets during the bankruptcy proceedings, the administrator shall investigate the same and inform the interested party of the results. If the administrator is unable to investigate or deems it unnecessary to do so, he shall give the reasons to the interested parties.

Article 132 Takeover of the debtor's assets

The administrator shall promptly take over the debtor's assets. With respect to any bank deposits transferred to the enforcement court, undistributed amount realized, actually seized movables and negotiable securities and other assets, the administrator shall, within five business days from the ascertainment date, bring the court order of acceptance of bankruptcy application, decision on the appointment of administrator and other legal documents with him, to go through the formalities with the enforcement court concerning the handover of such assets. Where coordination is needed, the administrator shall apply to the Court accepting the bankruptcy application in a timely manner.

Article 133 Payment of related expenses incurred under the enforcement proceedings

In cases where a bankruptcy application is accepted by the Court, expenses incurred under the enforcement proceedings shall be disbursed from the debtor's assets at any time, pursuant to the provisions concerning bankruptcy costs under the Enterprise Bankruptcy Law. Examples of such expenses include compulsory liquidation costs unpaid by the debtor, as well as evaluation fees, announcement fees and storage charges incurred in any ongoing enforcement proceedings.

Article 134 Time limit for filing of claims and preparation of the form of claims under summary proceedings

Where cases transferred from enforcement to bankruptcy proceedings are processed by summary procedures, the administrator shall inspect the claims and prepare the form of claims within five business days from the expiry of the prescribed time limit for filing of claims.

Article 135 Creditors' meetings where summary procedures are applied to bankruptcy cases transferred from enforcement to bankruptcy proceedings

Where cases transferred from enforcement to bankruptcy proceedings are processed by summary procedures, creditors' meetings are generally held in writing, without establishing a creditors' committee or appointing a chairman for the creditors' meeting.

Where cases transferred from enforcement to bankruptcy proceedings are processed by summary procedures, the administrator shall convene the first creditors' meeting in writing within seven business days from the expiry of the prescribed time limit for filing of claims. He shall also send the meeting materials to creditors and debtors two business days prior to the meeting, and file with the court for record.

Article 136 Voting in writing

In case of voting in writing, creditors shall be informed of the same on ballot papers: Any objection to the matter to be voted on shall be raised in writing within the voting period. Failure to cast a vote within the prescribed period will be considered to have voted affirmative.

Article 137 Time limits for voting and verification of claims

Where cases transferred from enforcement to bankruptcy proceedings are processed by summary procedures, time limits for voting and verification of claims do not, generally, exceed five days from the date of the creditors' meeting.

Article 138 Administrator's obligation to assist after the debtor being declared bankrupt

Upon receipt of the order and the announcement declaring the debtor's bankruptcy, the administrator shall, within three business days, assist the court to serve the order on the debtor, notify the known creditors and announce the same.

Article 139 Validity period of an appraisal report

The administrator may use any asset appraisal report issued under the enforcement proceedings. If an appraisal report is within one year from its expiry date, the administrator may, upon the consent of the court, request the original appraisal agency to issue a supplementary report or give explanations. If an appraisal report is at least one year from its expiry date, he shall apply for a reappraisal.

Article 140 Disposition of assets whose auction or sale has already been initiated under the enforcement proceedings

The assets whose auction or sale has already been initiated under the enforcement proceedings should be disposed of in the following manner:

(i) If the auction of an asset proves abortive or the asset fails to be sold off even at reduced price, or if the auction or sale is postponed or suspended, the administrator may, after taking control of such assets, continue to organize auctions or sales using the original reserve prices or selling prices.

(ii) Upon close of a successful auction or sale, if the award of auction has not been served onto the buyer, the administrator shall take over the auctioned or sold assets, along with the money realized therefrom. After taking over such assets, the administrator shall issue an auction/sale certificate according to the results of the auction or sale conducted under the enforcement proceedings, and shall then go through the delivery procedures.

(iii) If the award of auction has been served onto the buyer, the administrator shall take control of the money realized from such auction or sale.

Chapter III Compulsory Liquidation

Section 1 General Provisions

Article 141 Period of duty performance for a liquidation team

Generally, a liquidation team shall perform its duties from the date of receiving the People's Court decision of its appointment until the time when the respondent is deregistered or the case is transferred to bankruptcy proceedings.

Article 142 Election and powers of the leader of a liquidation team

The leader of a liquidation team may be appointed by the People's Court directly or after being elected by the group members at the request of the Court.

The head of a liquidation team shall exercise the functions and powers of the legal representative of the respondent.

Article 143 Replacement of members of a liquidation team

The Court may replace any member of a liquidation team at the request of creditors, the respondent's shareholders, directors or other interested persons, or according to its authority, if the member:

(i) has committed any offence against the law or administrative regulations;

(ii) has lost his professional capabilities or is incapacitated for civil acts; or

(iii) has committed any act seriously detrimental to the respondent or creditors.

Article 144 Remuneration of liquidation team members

The remuneration of liquidation team members shall be determined through consultation between the members and the respondent. If such consultation fails, the Court shall decide the same pursuant to the Provisions of the Supreme People's Court on Determining the Remuneration of Administrators for Processing Enterprise Bankruptcy Cases.

Article 145 Duties of a liquidation team

During the liquidation period, a liquidation team has the following duties:

(i) To discharge the taxes and social insurance contributions due by the respondent, as well as those incurred in the liquidation process;

(ii) To manage and dispose of the respondent's assets, and dispose of any residual assets of the latter, remaining after the repayment of all debts; and

(iii) To submit liquidation reports to the Court.

In addition to the duties prescribed in paragraph 1 of this article and other duties that may be required by the Court, the liquidation team shall also perform its duties with reference to those of the administrator.

Section 2 Scope of Work of a Liquidation team

Article 146 Time Limit for Notices and Announcements

A liquidation team shall notify known creditors in writing within ten days of its constitution and publicly announce the same within sixty days.

Article 147 Contents of notices and announcements

Such notices and announcements shall include:

(i) The date of constitution of a liquidation team, along with the names, addresses, telephone numbers of the group members; and

(ii) Proof of claims and other documents required for lodgment of claims.

Article 148 Preparing an asset report

After investigating the assets of the respondent, the liquidation team shall prepare a report on the status of such assets. It shall solicit opinions, through shareholders' meetings or shareholders' general meetings, on the report and then submit it to the Court.

In the absence of any shareholders' meeting or shareholders' general meeting, the liquidation team may submit the respondent's asset report directly to the Court.

Article 149 Adoption of preservation measures and restrictions on business activities

After the Court accepts an application for compulsory liquidation, the liquidation team may apply to the Court for taking preservation measures against the loss or damage of any asset of the respondent, if such asset is found to have been concealed, transferred, damaged or otherwise disposed of, undermining its legal liquidation. During the compulsory liquidation period, the respondent still has legal personality, but may not conduct business activities irrelevant to the liquidation. When the liquidation team decides to carry out business activities related to compulsory liquidation, it shall submit its decision to the Court for approval.

Chapter III Compulsory Liquidation

Article 150 Handling of executory contracts

A liquidation team, upon its constitution, shall decide to terminate or continue the performance of any executory contracts signed by the respondent with any other party prior to the dissolution of the respondent, and shall notify the other contracting party of its decision.

Article 151 Handling of certain affairs after the termination of a contract

Where the other contracting party is entitled to claim liability for breach of contract due to the termination thereof, it may lodge claims against the respondent. If that party has the right to recover the asset, the liquidation team shall deliver the same without delay.

If the other contracting party is in debt or obligated to hand over an asset to the respondent due to the termination of a contract, the liquidation team shall timely request the former to pay off the debt or hand over the asset. It shall protect the lawful rights of the respondent through litigation, arbitration or other means, if the other party fails to perform its obligations within a reasonable time limit.

Article 152 Measures to recover debts

After taking custody of the respondent, the liquidation team shall notify debtors of the respondent in writing to timely discharge debts with the group. Such a notice shall set forth, among others, particulars of the Court's acceptance of the application for compulsory liquidation and appointment of a liquidation team, the amount of debt payable by a debtor of the respondent, the time limit and methods for discharging debts, and the legal liability for not paying off debts. If a debtor of the respondent refuses to pay off his debts, the liquidation team may file a lawsuit or an arbitration in the name of the respondent according to law.

Article 153 Recovery of pledged collateral and assets encumbered with liens

After taking custody of the respondent's assets, the liquidation team may recover any pledged collateral or asset encumbered with a lien, by redeeming the relevant debts or providing alternative security acceptable to creditors.

Where the liquidation team, for the purpose of recovering any pledged or encumbered asset, discharges the relevant debts or provides alternative security acceptable to the creditor, the amount of security provided shall be to the extent of the market value of the pledged or encumbered asset at the time of pledge or encumbrance, if the value of such an asset is less than the amount of the secured claim.

Article 154 Right of set-off

Where a creditor makes a claim for set-off to a liquidation team, the latter shall decide whether to approve the set-off or not.

The claims made by a creditor to set off his debts to the respondent shall be authentic, valid and consistent with the Civil Code of the PRC and other laws and regulations, which shall also be confirmed upon submission.

Article 155 Exercise and enforcement of security interests

In compulsory liquidation proceedings, a creditor enjoying a security interest in any asset of the respondent may claim to exercise such interest. The discharge of security interests shall not be affected by the said proceedings.

Article 156 Claims not subject to compulsory liquidation

The following claims are not subject to compulsory liquidation:

(i) Expenses incurred by creditors for participating in liquidation proceedings;

(ii) Claims submitted by creditors to the liquidation team after the closure of compulsory liquidation proceedings;

(iii) Claims filed after the expiry of the relevant limitation periods, as well as the claims whose compulsory enforcement has not been applied within the time limit prescribed by law;

(iv) Funds or subsidies granted free of charge by the government to the respondent; and

(v) Other claims not subject to compulsory liquidation according to law.

The liquidation team shall also record the claims not subject to compulsory liquidation on the register of claims.

Article 157 Submission of claims involving pending actions or arbitration

Creditors may submit claims involving pending actions or arbitration initiated prior to the Court's decision to accept a liquidation application against the respondent.

Article 158 Formulation of a liquidation plan

After liquidating the assets of the respondent, preparing the balance sheet and the schedule of assets, the liquidation team shall formulate a liquidation plan. It shall solicit opinions, through shareholders' meetings or shareholders' general meetings, on the plan and then submit the plan to the Court for confirmation. The group shall not carry out the plan unless confirmed by the Court.

In the absence of any shareholders' meeting or shareholders' general meeting, the liquidation team may submit a liquidation plan directly to the Court for approval.

Article 159 Means to dispose of assets

The liquidation team shall dispose of the assets of the respondent through auctions or sales at reduced prices. If such assets are disposed of by other means, the group shall first solicit opinions through shareholders' meetings or shareholders' general meetings and then obtain approval from the Court.

In the absence of any shareholders' meeting or shareholders' general meeting, the liquidation team may directly file an application for using other disposal means with the Court for approval.

Article 160 Order of priority for distributing proceeds from liquidated assets

The proceeds from liquidated assets shall be used to pay the following in order: liquidation expenses, employees' salaries, social insurance contributions, statutory severance, and unpaid taxes. Any residual asset, remaining after discharging the debts owed by the respondent, shall be distributed to the shareholders in proportion to their capital contributions, if the respondent is a limited liability company. The same shall be distributed to the shareholders in proportion to their shareholdings if the respondent is a joint stock limited company. Where the distribution is otherwise agreed upon in the articles of association of a limited liability company or by its shareholders, such agreement shall prevail.

Article 161 Means to distribute proceeds from liquidated assets

Generally, proceeds from liquidated assets shall be distributed in cash in a lump sum. Distribution in kind may be made upon approval by shareholders accounting for at least 50% of the total voting rights at a shareholders' meeting, or by at least 50% shareholders with voting rights present at a general meeting of shareholders.

Any residual asset, remaining after discharging the debts owed by the respondent, may be distributed in kind upon approval by shareholders accounting for at least 50% of the total voting rights at a shareholders' meeting, or by at least 50% shareholders with voting rights present at a general meeting of shareholders.

Article 162 Satisfaction of conditional claims

With respect to a conditional claim or a claim whose rescission is contingent upon certain conditions, the liquidation team shall reserve the corresponding share of distribution. It may negotiate with a contingent creditor to determine the early satisfaction of the attached conditions, if doing so benefits the respondent, without detriment to other creditors.

The reserved amount mentioned above shall be distributed to the respondent's shareholders, if the attached conditions are unsatisfied or the rescission conditions are met prior to the final distribution of the respondent's assets. On the contrary, such amount shall be distributed to the creditor concerned, if the attached conditions are satisfied or the rescission conditions are not met.

Article 163 Treatment of proceeds uncollected by creditors

The liquidation team shall take custody of a creditor's share of asset distribution uncollected by the latter. Where the creditor still fails to collect his share when the group is close to disbandment, the group shall, in accordance with Article 570 of the Civil Code, deposit the uncollected asset at a notary office before its disbandment.

After depositing, the liquidation team shall perform its obligation of notification in accordance with Article 572 of the Civil Code of the PRC.

Article 164 Treatment of claims involving actions or arbitration pending

The liquidation team shall take custody of a creditor's share of distribution of the respondent's asset, if his claim involving any action or arbitration pending. Such a share may be handed over the creditor concerned or distributed to shareholders in line with the relevant court judgment or arbitral award.

Section 3 Execution and Termination of a Liquidation Plan

Article 165 Termination of liquidation proceedings

After completing the liquidation of a respondent, the liquidation team shall prepare a liquidation report, which shall be submitted to a shareholders' meeting, shareholders' general meeting or the Court for confirmation, and then to the registration authority of the respondent to apply for deregistration. Thereafter, the dissolution of the respondent should be announced.

In cases of compulsory liquidation where any principal asset, account book and crucial document of the respondent is lost or the whereabouts of the respondent is unknown, some debts may not be liquidated or fully liquidated even after the relevant situation has been explained to the respondent's shareholders, directors and other directly responsible persons, or after civil sanction measures such as fines have been taken. Under such circumstance, if partial liquidation of any existing assets may be made according to the existing account books and crucial documents, an equitable liquidation shall be made pursuant to the Enterprise Bankruptcy Law; thereafter, the compulsory liquidation proceedings shall be terminated on the grounds that a full liquidation cannot be done. In the absence of any asset, account book or crucial document and the ignorance of the respondent's whereabouts, such proceedings shall be terminated on the grounds that no liquidation is able to be carried out.

The liquidation team shall, upon the accomplishment of the lawful liquidation of the respondent, prepare a liquidation report and submit it to the Court for confirmation. The Court shall, upon confirmation, enter a ruling to terminate the liquidation proceedings.

Chapter III Compulsory Liquidation

Article 166 Insufficiency of debtor's assets to pay off its debts

While liquidating the respondent's assets, preparing its balance sheet and schedule of assets, the liquidation team may draw up debt composition plans upon negotiating with creditors if the respondent's assets are found to be insufficient to discharge its debts. Alternatively, it may file for bankruptcy according to Article 187 of the Company Law and Article 7(3) of the Enterprise Bankruptcy Law.

If a debt composition plan has been confirmed by all creditors and does not bring harm to other interested persons, the liquidation team shall notify the shareholders' meeting or shareholders' general meeting and report to the Court for approval. After the debts are discharged in accordance with the said plan, a liquidation report may be prepared and submitted to the Court for approval, which may terminate the liquidation proceedings as requested.

If the said plan fails to be confirmed by the creditors or approved by the shareholders' meeting or the shareholders' general meeting, the liquidation team shall file a bankruptcy application to the Court according to law.

Article 167 Transfer from compulsory liquidation to bankruptcy liquidation proceedings

After the Court's decision to accept the bankruptcy application filed by the respondent, the liquidation team shall turn over the liquidation affairs to the administrator designated by the Court.

A member of the liquidation team, if included in the list of administrators maintained by the People's Court accepting the bankruptcy case, may accept the appointment of the Court as an administrator of the case.

The liquidation team shall timely hand over the liquidation affairs and the relevant materials to the administrator. Matters already processed in the compulsory liquidation, if not inconsistent with the Enterprise Bankruptcy Law and relevant judicial interpretations, shall also have legal effect in the bankruptcy liquidation proceedings.

Chapter IV Individual Bankruptcy

Section 1 Selection and Appointment of Administrators

Article 168 Recommendation of candidates for the administrator

A creditor may, separately or jointly with other creditors, choose a candidate from the list of administrators for individual bankruptcy cases, and recommend the candidate to the Court. Where the Court designates the administrator as recommended by the creditor, the administrator may submit the schedule of work and budget to his recommender and is entitled to require the latter to prepay the expenses for performing his duties. If the recommender is unwilling to pay upfront, the administrator may refuse to accept the recommendation.

Article 169 Regime concerning a head of administrators

In case that the candidates recommended by different creditors are not the same, the Court may appoint one administrator from among them. The Court may appoint more than one administrator, considering the complexity of a case, the huge amount of the debtor's assets or the different locations of such assets. In that case, the administrators may jointly recommend a person in charge, who may be also designated by the Court.

Article 170 Recommendation from the bankruptcy administration authority

Where creditors fail to recommend a candidate for the administrator or the recommended candidate is held by the Court as unfit for the position, the Court shall notify the bankruptcy administration authority to propose and recommend new candidates. Such a candidate may not accept the recommendation without any necessary guarantee for performance of his duties.

Section 2 Investigation of the Debtor's Assets

Article 171 Verification and scope of a debtor's assets

The administrator shall inspect the assets filed by a debtor and may investigate the same according to the clues provided by creditors. The debtor's assets include any asset owned by the debtor at the time when the Court accepts the bankruptcy application, as well as any asset acquired by the debtor before the Court releases the debtor from all outstanding debts in accordance with relevant provisions.

The administrator shall primarily inspect the assets and interest in the assets in the name of the debtor, or a spouse, minor child or any other close relatives living together of the debtor, and require the debtor to truthfully file the following:

(i) Salary income, compensation for services, bank deposits, cash, funds in third-party payment platform accounts, amount of housing provident fund and other monetary assets;

(ii) Interests in property as a result of investing in or otherwise holding stocks, funds, investment-oriented insurance and other financial and wealth management products;

(iii) Interests from investment in any domestic or foreign non-listed joint stock limited company, limited liability company, registered individual business, sole proprietorship enterprise, partnership business and others;

(iv) Intellectual property rights, trust beneficiary rights, dividends from collective economic entities and other property rights and interests;

(v) Land use rights, housings, or any other property held in separate or common ownership;

(vi) Means of transport, machinery and equipment, products, raw materials and other property;

(vii) Personal collection of antiquities, calligraphy, paintings and other valuables;

(viii) Interests in assets lawfully held by the debtor through means of, among others, succession, gifting and nominee holding;

(ix) Expected assets and interests in assets for the debtor before the bankruptcy application is accepted;

(x) Other assets and interests in assets with disposal value.

The administrator shall also require the debtor to truthfully file overseas assets, together with interests in overseas assets which are of the same category as mentioned in the preceding paragraph.

Article 172 Special circumstances about the debtor's assets

Where a debtor falls under any of the following circumstances when filing asset and interests in assets, the administrator shall require the debtor to give explanations at the time of filing:

(i) The asset or interest in asset is owned by an adult child of the debtor, who, however, is a minor at the time of acquisition of such asset or interest;

(ii) The debtor's asset has been leased out or encumbered with security interests or other rights, or there is a co-owner or a dispute over the ownership of the asset;

(iii) The movable of the debtor is in the possession of a third party; or

(iv) An immovable, a particular movable or any other interest in asset of the debtor is registered in the name of a third party.

Article 173 Special changes to a debtor's assets

If any of the following changes occurs to a debtor's assets within two years prior to the date of the Court's decision to accept a bankruptcy application, the administrator shall require the debtor to file such changes together with the application:

(i) Gifting, transferring or leasing of an asset;

(ii) Creating a security interest or any other encumbrance on an asset;

(iii) Renouncing a claim or prolong the time limit for repayment of a claim;

(iv) Making a lump-sum payment of 50,000 yuan or above;

(v) Having community property divided in a divorce;

Chapter IV Individual Bankruptcy

(vi) Prepaying any undue debt;

(vii) Other major changes to property;

The administrator shall record, investigate, verify, and give opinions on any change to the debtor's assets as informed by a creditor or a third party.

Article 174 Determination of the scope of exempt assets

Exempt assets are those which the debtor is able to keep in accordance with the relevant bankruptcy laws and regulations, for the purpose of ensuring the basic living standard and rights of the debtor and his dependents. Such assets include:

(i) Essentials and reasonable expenses for the living, education and medical care of the debtor and his spouse, dependents and parents;

(ii) Essentials and reasonable expenses that shall be kept as required by the debtor's career development;

(iii) Items possessing special commemorative value to the debtor;

(iv) Non-cash value life insurance;

(v) Medals or other awards of honor;

(vi) Damages for personal injury, social insurance contribution and money for ensuring minimum living standard solely for the debtor; and

(vii) Other assets that should not be used for repayment of debts according to law or as required by public order, morals or good customs.

An asset mentioned in the preceding paragraph may not be treated as an exempt asset, if it has a relatively large value and its exemption obviously violates the principle of fairness or good faith.

The cumulative total of the exempt assets other than those under subparagraphs 5 and 6, paragraph 1 of this Article, shall not exceed 200,000 yuan in value. Where the debtor has sufficient evidence to prove that such value should be raised for the sake of treating serious diseases suffered by the debtor, his spouse, parents or children, the debtor shall file an application before the administrator. Upon the administrator's verification, the application shall be submitted to a creditors' meeting for deliberation and then to the Court for approval. If approved, the total value may be increased accordingly.

Article 175 Treatment of the list of exempt assets

The administrator shall, within thirty days from the date when the debtor files the schedule of his assets and the list of exempt assets, prepare the debtor's asset report upon examination and remark on the said list, which shall then be submitted to a creditors' meeting for a vote. If the list has not been adopted by the creditors' meeting through voting, the Court shall make a ruling.

Article 176 Obligation of assistance assumed by the relevant persons of the debtor

The administrator may request the debtor's spouse, parents, adult children and other interested parties to assist in the investigation. When inquiring into such persons, the administrator shall have two investigators present and keep records, which shall be signed by the two parties concerned upon confirmation.

Chapter IV Individual Bankruptcy

Section 3   Taking over and Disposing of the Debtor's Assets

Article 177 Takeover of the debtor's assets

Unless the Court orders that the debtor shall enter reorganization proceedings, the administrator shall timely take over all assets of the debtor except the exempt ones.

Article 178 Disposition of collateral

The obligee possessing a security interest to a particular asset of the debtor may, at any time, claim repayment in priority in respect of that asset. The administrator shall promptly realize such asset upon request; he shall not refuse such claims on the grounds that the resolution of a creditors' meeting is required in such circumstances. Where the administrator proposes that a secured asset be disposed in conjunction with other assets in bankruptcy, considering the value of other assets would be undermined by a separate disposal of the secured asset, the interests of the security interest holder shall not be substantially affected by such disposition.

When disposing of a secured asset, the administrator shall not harm the legitimate interests of the security interest holder, other creditors or title holders.

If a secured claim cannot be fully satisfied when the security interest holder exercises priority of being repaid, the unsatisfied portion of the claim shall be regarded as a general claim. Where the interest holder waives such priority, his claim shall be considered as a general claim. The remaining proceeds from the collateral left after repaying the interest holder, if any, shall be paid off collectively to general creditors.

The administrator may deduct the preservation and realization expenses payable by the security interest holder, such as those incurred by safekeeping, evaluation, auction, litigation and arbitration. The cost of realizing the security interest shall be limited to the actual expenditure.

Article 179 Right to revoke bankruptcy

The administrator may request the Court to revoke a bankruptcy, if the debtor, within two years prior to the filing of a bankruptcy application, disposes his assets in the following manner:

(i) Gifting his assets or interest in assets to any other person or entity, except those donated to social welfare causes or to fulfill moral obligations such as those donated to poverty alleviation and disaster relief programs, or such gifting is contingent upon obligations, which have been performed by the receiver as agreed;

(ii) Conducting a transaction on conspicuously unreasonable terms;

(iii) Securing an unsecured debt;

(iv) Creating a right of habitation on a property of the debtor in favor of any other person;

(v) Prepaying any undue debt;

(vi) Remitting a debt, or maliciously extending the period for performance of a claim as the claim becomes due; and

(vii) Providing security in favor of a third party other than a relative or an interested person.

Where the debtor has conclusive evidence to prove that no cause of bankruptcy has occurred at the time of disposition, and revocation of disposition will seriously interfere with the legitimate rights and interests of a third party, or will go against good public order, morals or good customs, the administrator may not exercise the revocation right.

If the administrator chooses not to exercise the revocation right, it shall report to the creditors' meeting and the Court.

Article 180 Handling of the debtor's discharge of debts owed to a few creditors

Where the debtor pays off a few creditors within six months upon filing for bankruptcy, or repays certain debts to his relatives and interested persons within two years upon bankruptcy filing, the administrator may request the Court to revoke such repayment, unless the payment:

(i) benefits the debtor's assets;

(ii) is essential for ensuring the normal life of the debtor;

(iii) is made by the debtor to satisfy a claim guaranteed by his own property, excluding where the value of the secured property at the time of repayment is less than the amount of the claim;

(iv) is made by the debtor by virtue of actions, arbitration or enforcement proceedings, excluding where the debtor and the creditor maliciously collude to harm the interests of other creditors.

Section 4 Representing the Debtor in Actions, Arbitration or Other Legal Proceedings

Article 181 Authority of the administrator to participate in actions or arbitration

If the administrator decides to (a) initiate a lawsuit or arbitration, or (b) during the legal process, withdraw the lawsuit or arbitration, reach a composition, or alter or waive his claims, he shall report to the Court for review in advance, and obtain consent from the creditors' meeting or creditors' committee when necessary.

Article 182 To participate in actions on behalf of the debtor

After the Court decides to accept a bankruptcy application and appoint an administrator, the administrator shall participate, on behalf of the debtor, in any civil action or arbitration pending or newly filed.

Chapter IV Individual Bankruptcy

Section 5 Handling of Special Circumstances Occurred to the Debtor

Article 183 Handling of the circumstance where the debtor is missing

If the whereabouts of the debtor is unknown after the Court accepts his filing of bankruptcy, the administrator shall report to the Court, proposing dismissal of the debtor's application.

Article 184 Handling of the circumstance where the debtor loses civil capacity

Where the debtor has been confirmed to have lost civil capacity through lawful procedures, the administrator shall urge his family members to determine a guardian for him, who shall participate in bankruptcy proceedings on behalf of the debtor.

Article 185 Handling of the circumstance where the debtor is dead

If the debtor dies after the Court's acceptance of bankruptcy application, the administrator shall solicit opinions from the heirs of the debtor. Where the heirs agree to continue the bankruptcy proceedings or there is no heir, the Court shall enter a ruling to terminate the bankruptcy proceedings after the administrator takes custody of and realizes the debtor's assets and then distributes the proceeds therefrom.

If the heirs of the debtor are inaccessible or fail to reach an agreement within thirty days upon the debtor's death, the Court shall enter a ruling to terminate the bankruptcy proceedings. The administrator shall deal with any relevant matters in accordance with the provisions of Civil Code on inheritance after the bankruptcy costs and debts incurred in the common interest of the creditors are discharged by using the legacy left by the debtor.

Section 6 Duties to Supervise the Debtor

Article 186 Administrator's general supervisory duties in bankruptcy proceedings

From the date of the Court's acceptance of a bankruptcy application to the date of Court order to discharge the debtor from any outstanding debts, the administrator shall supervise the debtor's performance of the following obligations:

(i) To submit or supplement relevant materials as required by the Court, the bankruptcy administration authority and the administrator, and cooperate with their investigation;

(ii) To attend creditors' meetings as a nonvoting member and answer inquiries;

(iii) To timely report to the bankruptcy administration authority and the administrator in the event that the debtor changes his name, contact information, address and other personal information, or needs to leave his place of residence;

(iv) To report to the administrator one month prior to his marriage or divorce;

(v) To refrain from travelling abroad without the consent of the People's Court;

(vi) To timely register and file with the Court and the bankruptcy administration authority major matters concerning individual bankruptcy, including but not limited to: a bankruptcy application, assets and liability status, a reorganization plan or composition agreements, and information on income and consumption during the bankruptcy proceedings;

(vii) To declare his bankruptcy status to a lender or credit grantor when obtaining a loan of not less than 1,000 yuan or applying for a line of credit at the same amount; and

(viii) To cooperate with the People's Court, the bankruptcy administration authority, and the administrator in other work in connection with the bankruptcy proceedings.

Article 187 Administrator's supervisory duties during the observation period for the debtor

During the observation period, a debtor shall register and file his personal income, expenditure, and assets status, as well as other data in the bankruptcy information system of the bankruptcy administration authority on a monthly basis.

During the observation period, the administrator shall supervise the debtor to see whether he has gone against the restrictions imposed on his behaviors and whether some of his behaviors have violated the principle of good faith; in addition, the administrator shall also examine the annual personal income, expenditure, and property report submitted by the debtor, and take custody of and distribute the debtor's new or newly discovered assets each year in accordance with the plan for distribution of assets in bankruptcy.

Article 188 Subject to supervision by the bankruptcy administration authority

The administrator shall adopt the reasonable suggestions put forward by the bankruptcy administration authority on the performance of his duties.

Where any interested person complains to the bankruptcy administration authority about the administrator's dereliction of duty or other illegal acts, the administrator shall truthfully report the situation and give the reasons therefor.

Section 7 Other Provisions

Article 189 Relationship and connection between individual and enterprise bankruptcy proceedings

In the absence of any applicable provision in this chapter, the pertinent provisions in Chapters II, V & VII hereof shall apply mutatis mutandis.

Chapter V Reorganization

Section 1 General Provisions

Article 190 Basic duties

Where the Court delivers an order that the debtor shall be reorganized, the administrator shall perform its duties in accordance with the provisions of Chapters Ⅰ, Ⅱ & Ⅴ hereof.

Section 2 Managing the Debtor's Assets and Business Affairs

Article 191 Informing the debtor of its right to manage its own assets and business affairs

After the Court orders a debtor to reorganize, the administrator may, as the case may be, inform the debtor of its right to apply to the Court for managing its assets and business affairs on its own.

Article 192 Hiring the debtor's operation team

Where the administrator is responsible for the management of the debtor's assets and business affairs, the administrator may, upon the Court's approval of his written application, hire the operation team and other staff members of the debtor to deal with its business affairs.

Where the administrator hires the debtor's operation team and other staff members to deal with its business affairs, the position and duties shall be fixed for each person, whose remuneration may be reasonably determined in line with the debtor's salary structure or the wage standard of a person in the same position, involved in the same industry in the area where the debtor is located.

Article 193 Entrusting an operation agency

As actually needed by the reorganization of the debtor, the administrator may, with the prior consent of a creditors' meeting or its authorized creditors' committee, and the approval of the Court, entrust a professional operation agency to handle the debtor's assets, business affairs and other related matters during the reorganization.

Article 194 Entrusting a professional firm

In the reorganization procedure, if the administrator truly needs to hire a professional firm to deal with the debtor's financial affairs, he may, with the approval of the Court, openly hire such a firm, and shall supervise the relevant conducts of the latter.

Article 195 Safe production

If the debtor needs to continue production during the reorganization period, the administrator shall, before approving the production, order the debtor to take necessary measures to ensure safe production, inspect whether its safe production facilities and conditions meet the requirements of the State, and then require the debtor to designate a person in charge of safe production.

If the debtor fails to meet the requirements for safe production imposed by competent government authorities even after rectification, the administrator shall timely cease all or the concerned production activities of the debtor to prevent accidents from happening.

Article 196 Performance or termination of executory contracts

If a debtor's reorganization falls under the circumstances envisaged in the Enterprise Bankruptcy Law, Article 70(1), the administrator shall have the right to terminate or continue the performance of any executory contract signed by the debtor before the court order of reorganization, provided that he shall notify the other contracting party. If the administrator fails to notify the other party within two months from the order of reorganization, or fails to reply within thirty days from the receipt date of the relevant notice issued by that party, the contract concerned shall be deemed terminated.

Where a debtor's reorganization falls under the circumstances envisaged in the Enterprise Bankruptcy Law, Article 70(2), any executory contract signed by the debtor before the Court's acceptance of the bankruptcy application shall be dealt with pursuant to the relevant provisions hereof.

If the administrator decides to continue the performance of a contract, the other party shall fulfill the contract, provided that the latter has the right to request the provision of security. If the administrator fails to do so, the contract shall be deemed terminated.

Article 197 Recovery of the debtor's assets

In the reorganization proceedings, if the debtor falls under the circumstances prescribed in Article 16, 31, 32 or 33 of the Enterprise Bankruptcy Law and Article 20 or 24 of the Provisions of the Supreme People's Court on Several Issues Concerning the Application of the Enterprise Bankruptcy Law (II), the administrator shall first investigate and then recover the assets through means like negotiation and litigation. Where it is necessary to suspend the recovery of the assets or to waive the right of recourse, he may do so only after a thorough review and analysis, and being approved by the creditors' meeting and the Court.

Article 198 Investigating the seizure and pledge of equity interests

During the reorganization period, the administrator shall report to the Court any encumbrance that he has found through investigation on the equity interests of the debtor's shareholders, such as pledge and preservation.

Article 199 Restrictions on equity transfer and income distribution by shareholders

Where the administrator finds that the debtor's shareholders distribute the income from their investment in violation of relevant rules or in any disguised form, he shall timely stop such distribution and may recover those already distributed. If any shareholder refuses to return the income, the administrator shall recover the same through litigation.

When a director, supervisor or senior executive of the debtor intends to transfer the debtor's equity to a third party, he shall apply to the administrator in advance. If the administrator, upon examination, holds that such a transfer has been included in the part of draft reorganization plan relating to the adjustment of contributors' interests and will not affect the progress of the reorganization proceedings, he shall apply to the Court for approval after the transfer is adopted at a creditors' meeting.

Article 200 Taking out loans to pay bankruptcy costs and debts incurred in the common interests of creditors

Prior to the first creditors' meeting, if the administrator takes out loans to pay bankruptcy costs and debts incurred in the common interests of creditors, and further to facilitate the reorganization proceedings, he shall file with the Court for approval and report to the first creditors' meeting. Where a loan is taken after the first creditors' meeting, the administrator shall first submit a report to a creditors' meeting for approval and then report the same to the Court.

Article 201 Creating security for business loans

If adopted at a creditors' meeting or approved by the Court before the first creditors' meeting, the administrator or the debtor (if it self-manages its business) may take out loans to continue the business of the debtor.

Where the administrator takes out a loan in the name of the debtor for the purpose of continuing its business, he may use the debtor's property as security for the loan. If the security is created prior to the first creditors' meeting, the administrator shall submit a plan to the Court for examination and approval; if it is created thereafter, the administrator shall submit the same to a creditors' meeting for examination and approval.

Where a debtor self-managing its property and business affairs takes out a loan or provides security for the loan before the first creditors' meeting, the administrator shall apply to the Court for examination and approval; where the same is done thereafter, the administrator shall apply to a creditors' meeting for examination and approval.

The debts incurred by loans taken for the purpose of continuing business operation may be paid in priority over general claims according to the Enterprise Bankruptcy Law, Article 42(2), unless otherwise specified in the reorganization plan or the secured creditor agrees to be pay off with the secured property.

Where the administrator or the self-managed debtor creates a security on a loan taken for the purpose of continuing its business, but nevertheless the collateral has already been mortgaged to other creditors before the acceptance of the bankruptcy application, the said secured debt shall be repaid in the order of priority prescribed in Article 414 of the Civil Code.

Article 202 Safekeeping of collateral

The administrator shall be responsible for the management and maintenance of collateral, and shall timely report in writing to the Court and the secured party if it finds that the collateral is likely to suffer damage or reduction in value serious enough to jeopardize the rights of the secured party.

Where the debtor self-manages its assets and business affairs, the administrator shall supervise the debtor to manage and maintain the collateral according to paragraph 1 of this Article.

Article 203 Restrictions on exercise of security interests

After the application for reorganization is accepted, the administrator or the self-managed debtor shall timely determine whether the debtor's secured asset is essential in the reorganization. After that, either of the parties shall timely auction any secured property that is not essential. The proceeds therefrom shall, after paying the auction expenses, be used to satisfy the corresponding secured claim in priority. If a debt needs to be paid off by sale of collateral at reduced price or discount, rather than auction, the administrator shall report, or supervise the self-managed debtor to report, to a creditors' meeting or its authorized creditors' committee and obtain the consent of the latter.

During the period when the exercise of security interest is suspended, the secured party shall, in accordance with Article 75 of the Enterprise Bankruptcy Law, apply to the Court for resuming the exercise of the interest. If the secured collateral is considered essential for reorganization, the administrator or the self-managed debtor shall produce relevant proof before the Court and provide security or compensation equivalent to the reduced value, so as to facilitate the Court to make a ruling according to law.

Where the administrator plans, in line with the requirements of the reorganization proceedings, to dispose of any asset of the debtor which may significantly affect the interests of creditors, he shall work out an asset management or realization plan in advance and submit it to a creditors' meeting for voting. Such disposition of assets includes recovering any pledged collateral or asset encumbered with a lien by discharging the relevant debt or providing alternative security, or paying off a debt by selling the collateral or encumbered asset at a discount. If the aforesaid plan fails to be adopted at a creditors' meeting, the administrator may not dispose of the asset in question. The administrator shall timely report to the creditors' committee before disposing of any asset. In the absence of a creditors' committee, the administrator shall promptly report to the Court.

Article 204 Resumption of the exercise of a security interest

Where the Court enters a ruling approving the exercise of a security interest upon the application of the interest holder, the administrator shall, upon receipt of the written ruling, formulate a realization plan for the secured asset in a timely manner. When making the plan, the administrator or the self-managed debtor shall adhere to the principle of maximizing the value of the debtor's asset, but also fully consider the opinions of the interest holder. If the secured asset is considered one of the debtor's major assets as stipulated in Enterprise Bankruptcy Law, Article 69(1), in addition to the submission of the realization plan to the creditors' meeting for voting, the disposition of the secured asset shall also be timely reported to the creditors' committee or the Court according to Enterprise Bankruptcy Law, Article 69(2).

Article 205 Redundancy during reorganization

During the period of reorganization, if the debtor needs to lay off more than twenty employees or above ten percent of its employees although the number is less than twenty, the administrator shall promptly report to the Court, and explain and listen to the trade union or all its staff thirty days in advance. Employees may be laid off after the redundancy plan is submitted to the labor administrative authority.

When the debtor is being downsized, the administrator shall retain the following employees in priority:

(i) Anyone who has a long-fixed term employment contract with the debtor;

(ii) Anyone who has an open-term employment contract with the debtor; and

(iii) The only bread earner in a family with elders or minors to be supported.

Section 3 Self-Management of the Debtor's Assets and Business Affairs

Article 206 Basic conditions for self-management

During the period of reorganization, if the debtor meets the following conditions, the administrator submits his written opinion to the People's Court and, the debtor may, upon the approval of the Court, manage its own assets and business affairs under the supervision of the administrator:

(i) When the People's Court accepts the bankruptcy application, the debtor keeps production and operation going, or satisfies the conditions to resume production although its production has been suspended;

(ii) The debtor's internal governance structure is sound enough to ensure its normal operation; and the self-management of the debtor is approved by its board of directors, shareholders' meeting or shareholders' general meetings;

(iii) The debtor has practical and feasible management measures in place, which are conducive to its continual operation;

(iv) The debtor does not otherwise act to the detriment of creditors;

(v) The debtor has not been found to be involved in concealment or transfer of its assets;

(vi) The administrator has worked out a supervision scheme;

(vii) Other conditions that the People's Court considers necessary.

Article 207 Handover of the debtor's assets and business affairs from the administrator to the debtor

During the reorganization period, upon the People's Court approval of the debtor's self-management of its assets and business affairs, the administrator, if having already taken custody of the debtor's assets and business affairs, shall hand over such assets and affairs back to the debtor without delay; if not having taken custody of the same yet, he shall stop doing so.

The administrator and the debtor shall timely specify their respective functions and powers upon discussion and then report to the People's Court. The debtor shall exercise certain powers and functions of the administrator, such as to prepare a draft reorganization plan and to manage its assets and business affairs. Other functions and powers should still be exercised by the administrator in principle. In case of any disagreement on their respective functions and powers, it shall be determined by the People's Court.

Article 208 Main duties of the debtor

Where the debtor manages its assets and business affairs by itself, the administrator shall inform the debtor to perform the following major duties:

(i) To be in charge of its business affairs;

(ii) To manage its assets, financial books, instruments and other materials;

(iii) To create an institutional framework for the daily management of the debtor and formulate relevant normative documents;

(iv) To decide the debtor's internal management affairs;

(v) To decide which employees of the debtor shall stay at their positions;

(vi) To determine daily and other necessary expenses according to its financial management system;

(vii) To report the status of its assets to creditors' meetings;

(viii) To subject to the supervision of the administrator, to whom the budget and final statements shall be submitted, and with whom the accounts shall be checked on a regular basis;

(ix) To prepare a draft reorganization plan and the supporting documents; and

(x) Other duties of the debtor as stipulated by relevant laws or supervision schemes;

The administrator shall, in line with his supervisory powers, supervise the debtor's self-management of its assets and business affairs.

Article 209 Range of duties performed by the administrator

Where the debtor is managed by itself, the administrator shall generally perform the following duties:

(i) To investigate the assets and liabilities of the debtor;

(ii) To record and examine the claims filed against the debtor, and to inspect claims for right of recovery and right of set-off;

(iii) To recover assets in accordance with Articles 31, 32, 33 & 36 of the Enterprise Bankruptcy Law;

(iv) To organize and convene meetings of creditors and meetings of interested persons;

(v) To participate on behalf of the debtor in pending actions, arbitration or other legal proceedings that have been initiated before the supervision period;

(vi) To supervise and urge the debtor to complete the draft reorganization plan on schedule;

(vii) To request the relevant persons of the debtor to assist and answer inquiries;

(viii) To supervise the management and use of the debtor's seals;

(ix) To supervise the debtor's financial income, expenditure and management;

(x) To supervise the debtor's property and operation safety; and

(xi) Other duties as required by the supervision scheme and the People's Court.

Article 210 Supervision over the debtor's self-management

Where the debtor applies to self-manage its assets and business affairs, the administrator shall timely formulate a plan for supervising the debtor's self-management and carry out the plan after reporting to the People's Court.

When the administrator exercises supervisory powers during the reorganization period, he shall report the relevant situation to the People's Court, the creditors' meeting and the creditors' committee. If it is found that the debtor has seriously harmed creditors' interests or is under any other circumstances where self-management is not an option, the administrator may apply to the Court for a ruling to terminate the self-management of the debtor.

If the People's Court decides to terminate the debtor's self-management, the administrator shall promptly take over the debtor's assets and business affairs.

Article 211 Supervision methods

The administrator's supervision over the debtor's self-management includes requiring the debtor to submit interim and also periodic reports.

"Interim report" refers to the report submitted, upon the request of the administrator, by the debtor to the People's Court, creditors' meetings or the creditors' committee when the debtor legally reports to such organizations its decision on matters that may seriously affect the interests of creditors. Such matters generally include the debtor's decision to continue or suspend its business activities before the first creditors' meeting, or any of the acts prescribed in Article 69 of the Enterprise Bankruptcy Law.

"Periodic report" refers to the report submitted, upon the request of the administrator, by the debtor to the administrator on a regular basis concerning the performance of duties under its own management.

When the administrator, in the performance of its supervisory functions, finds that the debtor has acted to the detriment of creditors, he shall promptly report to the creditors' committee. In the absence of a creditors' committee, he shall report to the People's Court.

Article 212 Asset preservation

During the period of reorganization, the administrator shall apply to the Court for measures to preserve all or part of the debtor's assets if the lawful progress of bankruptcy proceedings may potentially be affected by any act of the interested persons or any other reason.

Article 213 Report on the debtor's management practices

During the self-management of the debtor, the debtor shall report to the administrator if it is necessary to dispose of its assets according to the Enterprise Bankruptcy Law, Article 69. The administrator shall handle the matter in accordance with the Provisions of the Supreme People's Court on Several Issues Concerning the Application of the Enterprise Bankruptcy Law of the People's Republic of China (III), Article 15.

Chapter V Reorganization

If the debtor needs to do something like changing its enterprise business or operation plan, or appointing or removing individuals to or from crucial positions, the debtor may do so according to its own decision, provided that it shall report to the administrator in advance. In case that its decision is disapproved by the administrator, it shall report to the People's Court.

Article 214 Principle of prior scrutiny and supervision

The administrator shall abide by the following principles in scrutinizing any significant act of the debtor, such as disposal of assets, change in business operation and appointment or removal of employees:

(i) The act is essential to the debtor's continuous production and operation, without detriment to the legal rights and interests of all creditors;

(ii) The act is indispensable to keeping the value of the debtor's reorganization; and

(iii) The act is conducive to realizing the legitimate rights and interests of all creditors.

Article 215 Circumstances requiring application for termination of self-management

Where any of the following circumstances occurs during the debtor's self-management, the administrator shall apply for termination of such self-management:

(i) The debtor has committed any act stipulated in Articles 31-33 of the Enterprise Bankruptcy Law;

(ii) The debtor, against the duty of good faith, maliciously reduces its assets, commits fraud or engages in any practice detrimental to the interests of all creditors;

(iii) The act of the debtor causes serious adverse consequences to its reorganization;

(iv) Creditors at a creditors' meeting are of the opinion that the debtor's self-management would harm the legal rights and interests of creditors, and a resolution forbidding the debtor from self-management is passed thereat;

(v) The debtor applies for revocation of the self-management permission; and

(iv) Other circumstances calling for discontinuing self-management of the debtor.

Where the Court decides to terminate the debtor's self-management, the administrator shall take over the debtor's assets and business affairs.

Section 4 Consolidated Reorganization of Related Debtor Companies

Article 216 Doctrine of cautious use

Bearing in mind the doctrine of honoring the independence of enterprise personality, the bankruptcies of related debtor companies shall be processed in different manners, taking into account the specific relationship between them.

In general, the basic principle is to evaluate the causes of bankruptcy separately for each related company, but to apply a single bankruptcy procedure to all of these companies. In case of substantial identity between the enterprise personalities of such companies, which renders the costs to distinguish the assets of each company prohibitive or seriously impairs creditors' interest of being repaid fairly, a substantive consolidation of such companies may be employed as an "extraordinary remedy".

Article 217 Conditions to use reorganization through substantive consolidation

A related debtor company, its contributor or creditor, or its administrator (if a bankruptcy procedure has been initiated), may apply for consolidated reorganization of multiple related companies that have causes for reorganization, and may also apply for putting these companies under a single reorganization procedure, if (a) there is substantial identity between the enterprise personalities of related debtor companies, which renders the costs to distinguish the assets of each company prohibitive, or seriously impairs creditors' interest of being repaid fairly, or (b) a substantive consolidation of these companies increases the possibility of reorganization and benefits all creditors of the related companies.

Article 218 Determination of substantial identity between enterprise personalities

If the related debtor companies are generally under the following circumstances on a continual basis, it may be held that there is substantial identity between their enterprise personalities:

(i) Their principal business assets are almost indistinguishable;

(ii) Their financial vouchers are almost indistinguishable or their accounts are used interchangeably;

(iii) Their premises are not clearly differentiated;

(iv) Their primary business is identical, and their transaction behaviors, modes, prices, among others, are controlled by a holding company;

(v) Practices of mutual guarantee or cross-shareholding are found among them;

(vi) Directors, supervisors or senior executives work alternately in these companies;

(vii) The related debtor companies are under the control of the same actual controller, where major decision-making issues, such as employee appointment and removal, and decisions in respect of operation and management, are not subject to necessary procedures; and

(viii) Other circumstances that result in the loss of independence of the assets of a related debtor company, as well as its inability to demonstrate its independent will.

Article 219 Hearing of reorganization through substantive consolidation

Where the applicant submit application for reorganization through substantive consolidation of the related debtor companies, the administrator shall assist the People's Court in timely notifying the interested parties.

Where any of the related debtor companies, its contributor or creditor raises objections thereto, the administrator shall assist the People's Court in organizing hearings and investigations as necessary.

Chapter V Reorganization

Article 220 Allocation of the burden of proof with respect to reorganization through substantive consolidation

The applicant shall provide factual evidence with respect to the reorganization application through substantive consolidation.

If the administrator applies for reorganization through substantive consolidation, he shall provide proof that there is substantial confusion of enterprise personalities among the related debtor companies, rendering the costs to distinguish the assets of each company prohibitive, or seriously impairs creditors' interest of being repaid fairly, or a substantive consolidation of these companies increases the possibility of reorganization and benefits all creditors.

Where an interested party applies for consolidated reorganization, the administrator may give his opinions on the basis of the proof submitted by the former.

Article 221 Reconsideration remedies

If the administrator is dissatisfied with the ruling entered by the People's Court with regards to reorganization through substantively consolidating the related debtor companies, he may apply for reconsideration to the People's Court superior to the one hearing the case within fifteen days upon receipt of the written ruling.

Article 222 Legal consequences of substantive consolidation

If the People's Court enters a ruling that the related debtor companies shall be substantively consolidated in reorganization, the claims and debts between these companies shall be extinguished, the assets of each related company shall be deemed unexceptionally the assets of the debtor, and the creditors of all related companies shall be fairly satisfied in the statutory order of repayment.

Where substantive consolidation of related companies is employed in reorganization, the draft reorganization plan shall contain uniform schemes for classification, adjustment and repayment of claims.

Article 223 Connection of proceedings

Where the People's Court enters a ruling that the related debtor companies shall be substantively consolidated in reorganization, the investigation, examination of claims filed, financial audit, asset evaluation and other work or procedures completed in the bankruptcy case of each related company prior to the consolidation shall remain effective.

Bankruptcy expenses and common interest debts incurred prior to the consolidation shall be regarded as those incurred in the case of reorganization through substantive consolidation.

After the Court rules that the related debtor companies shall be substantively consolidated for hearing, the deadline for submitting a draft reorganization plan may be rescheduled.

Section 5 Reorganization Investors

Article 224 Recruiting prospective reorganization investors

Where the debtor self-manages its assets and business affairs, it may bring in reorganization investors by means of, among others, negotiation, targeted invitation and open recruitment.

After the convening of the first creditors' meeting or the issuance of an order to reorganize the debtor in bankruptcy liquidation, if the debtor fails to timely propose a feasible plan for debt repayment and future business operation, the administrator may bring in reorganization investors through open recruitment, acceptance of recommendation, invitation for consultation, and other channels.

Where the administrator is responsible for management of the debtor's assets and business affairs, he may bring in reorganization investors through means like open recruitment and targeted invitation. Alternatively, he may do so through negotiation on the basis of the recommendation made by creditors.

Article 225 Open recruitment process and preparation of recruitment documents

Where the administrator openly recruits reorganization investors, he may initiate the process immediately after the debtor's assets are appraised. He may also do so in advance according to the actual situation of the reorganization case.

Relevant procedures shall be initiated in a timely manner, if the administrator decides to publicly recruit investors for reorganization when the People's Court orders to reorganize the debtor after accepting its application for bankruptcy liquidation but before declaring it bankrupt.

The administrator shall prepare recruitment documents prior to the recruitment announcement, and file them with the People's Court upon the consent of the creditors' committee. Such documents shall include the basic information of the debtor's assets and liabilities, the requirement on security deposits payable by prospective investors, the documents required from prospective investors and the submission deadline, the standards and procedures for selecting reorganization investors, and the specific requirements for an investor and its reorganization plan.

Article 226 Application for determining reorganization investors through negotiations

The administrator may apply to determine reorganization investors through negotiations if any of the following circumstances is found upon examination:

(i) The debtor and the prospective investor have preliminarily formulated a feasible debt repayment plan and a contributors' equity adjustment plan during the period of the debtor's self-management;

(ii) When the application for reorganization is accepted, the debtor has earmarked some prospective reorganization investors, who have kept providing the debtor with funds for the purpose of continuing its business and satisfying the claims of its employees, and have also worked out with the debtor a feasible debt repayment plan and a contributors' equity adjustment plan;

(iii) The reorganization investors need to be determined with the least delay possible as the value of reorganization is likely to lose sharply; or

(iv) There are other circumstances where an open recruitment of reorganization investors is not an option as agreed by a creditors' meeting or creditors' committee.

Article 227 Selection of investors

During the recruitment period, investors shall, according to the standards and procedures for selecting reorganization investors in the recruitment document, be selected from all the prospective investors who have submitted the required documents and are deemed eligible upon examination.

Article 228 Announcement of open recruitment

Where reorganization investors are to be openly recruited, the administrator shall post a recruitment announcement with a period of no less than fifteen days on the National Enterprise Bankruptcy Information Disclosure Platform, nationwide or industrywide influential media or other platforms.

The recruitment announcement shall clearly include:

(i) Basic information of the case;

(ii) Qualification requirements for prospective investors;

(iii) How to register for the recruitment process and the deadline; and

(iv) How to obtain the recruitment documents and the deadline.

Article 229 Disclosure of reorganization information

The administrator may, in accordance with the agreement with a reorganization investor, disclose the following information of the debtor to the latter:

(i) Information on the debtor's assets and business status;

(ii) Details of actions and/or arbitration involving the debtor; and

(iii) Other information requested by the investor.

Article 230 Protection of the interests of reorganization investors

At the request of reorganization investors, provisions on the protection of their rights and interests may be incorporated into the draft reorganization plan. If investors hope to obtain policy support from the local government, the administrator may provide assistance.

Section 6   Preparation, Adoption and Approval of the Reorganization Plan

Article 231 Preparer of a draft reorganization plan

If the debtor self-manages its assets and business affairs, the debtor shall prepare a draft reorganization plan. The administrator shall offer opinions on the legality and feasibility thereof upon analysis, and report to the People's Court in writing before the plan is submitted to a creditors' meeting for a vote.

Where the administrator is responsible for the management of the debtor's assets and business affairs, the administrator shall prepare a draft reorganization plan.

Article 232 Basic requirements for preparing a draft reorganization plan

In a draft reorganization plan, the same class of claims shall be treated equally, with priority claims being repaid before any other claims. All creditors, including dissenting creditors, shall receive the repayment they are entitled to in the bankruptcy proceedings. The arrangements in the draft should be feasible, in particular the debtor's business plan.

Article 233 Submission deadline for a draft reorganization plan and application for an extension

The administrator or the debtor shall submit a draft reorganization plan to the People's Court and a creditors' meeting within six months from the date when the Court orders the debtor to reorganize. The Court may, at the request of the administrator or the debtor on justifiable grounds, order an extension of three months beyond the period mentioned above. If the draft preparation is impacted by any major action or arbitration pending, it may be proposed to the People's Court that the period of such action or arbitration be excluded from the submission period.

If the administrator applies for an extension, he shall submit a written application to the People's Court ten days prior to the expiration of the submission period and state the reasons. Where the debtor applies for an extension, the administrator shall submit supervisory opinions to the Court on whether the application is justified.

Article 234 Requirements for a self-managed debtor in respect to submission of a draft reorganization plan

If a self-managed debtor fails to submit a draft reorganization plan within the last month before the expiration of the submission period, the administrator may propose a draft plan within the statutory period, which shall also be submitted to the People's Court and a creditors' meeting.

Where the draft reorganization plan submitted by a self-managed debtor is considered illegal or conspicuously infeasible by the Court, or disapproved by a voting group, the administrator may propose a draft plan within the statutory period.

Article 235 Communication prior to drawing up a draft reorganization plan

In the process of formulating a draft reorganization plan, the administrator shall fully listen to creditors, debtors, reorganization investors, contributors and other parties concerned, and may call for consultation and discussion among them if necessary. The aforementioned parties are encouraged to engage professional firms to render pertinent suggestions to the draft preparer for reference.

Article 236 Statements on drawing up a draft reorganization plan

When drawing up a draft reorganization plan, the administrator may simultaneously prepare a statement thereon to expound on the debtor's business plan, claims classification, claims adjustment plan, claims repayment plan, implementation period of the reorganization plan, the period for supervising the implementation of the reorganization plan and other schemes conducive to the debtor's reorganization.

When a draft reorganization plan is being voted on at a creditors' meeting, the administrator shall explain the draft and answer inquiries at the meeting.

Article 237 Contents of a draft reorganization plan

In addition to the particulars under Paragraphs 1 to 7, Article 81 of the Enterprise Bankruptcy Law, a draft reorganization plan may also cover causes for the debtor's bankruptcy, status of its assets and liabilities, analysis of solvency, and the major uncertainties concerning the debtor's assets.

If any adjustment of contributors' equity is involved, the draft reorganization plan shall be prepared upon negotiation with the contributors and the pledgees who have the right to enforce the pledged equity.

Article 238 Calculation of repayment proportion

With respect to general claims which cannot be paid off in full in the reorganization proceedings, the administrator shall calculate himself, or hire a professional firm to calculate the proportion of such claims that may be discharged in accordance with the bankruptcy liquidation procedure. And such calculation shall be included in a draft reorganization plan.

Article 239 Grouping of voting

In principle, a draft reorganization plan shall be voted on in groups according to the classes of claims set out under the Enterprise Bankruptcy Law, Article 82, Paragraph 1. The administrator may, as the case may be, request the creation of voting groups.

With the consent of the Court, claims granted statutory priority may be grouped with secured claims in the voting process, or another voting group may be set up particularly in line with the nature of the priority.

Claims for damages for personal injury caused by the debtor's infringement, except the punitive damages involved, may be voted on by the voting group set forth in Article 82, Paragraph 1, Subparagraph 2 of the Enterprise Bankruptcy Law.

Claims for social insurance contributions unpaid by the debtor, other than debts owed to the employees, may not be voted on in groups.

The administrator may, when necessary, request the People's Court to decide to set up a subgroup of small claims within the group of general claims for voting. The criteria for grouping may be determined by considering the amount of claims, the proportion of repayment, and other factors.

Article 240 Setting up a group of contributors

If a draft reorganization plan involves the adjustment of contributors' equity, a group of contributors shall be set up to vote on the matter.

In case of voting on the adjustment of contributors' equity, a group meeting of contributors shall be convened and all contributors shall be notified fifteen days in advance. If such a meeting is not called, a vote may be done by collecting the written ballot of each contributor.

Should the group of contributors of a listed company, or any other public company with a large number of shareholders, vote on a draft reorganization plan, it may be carried out virtually, physically or through other means. The online voting rights shall be exercised in accordance with the relevant provisions issued by China Securities Regulatory Commission.

If a shareholders' meeting or shareholders' general meeting of the debtor has already adopted a resolution on the adjustment of contributors' equity, a vote may not be otherwise cast by a separate group meeting of contributors.

Article 241 Amount of a secured claim for voting

If the value of a secured property is assessed to be insufficient to repay a secured claim, the assessed value may be treated as the amount of the claim for voting in the group of secured claims, with the residual amount as the one for voting in the group of general claims.

Article 242 Nonvoting participants in creditors' meetings

Representatives of the debtor's contributors may attend as nonvoting participants at a creditors' meeting where a draft reorganization plan is discussed.

A pledgee enjoying the right to enforce any pledged equity held by a contributor or an applicant who has applied for judicial enforcement measures against such equity may attend the said meetings as stakeholders.

Article 243 Voting methods

Voting on a draft reorganization plan may be conducted physically or non-physically. The voting process is generally carried out in the following order:

(i) The administrator or the debtor introduces a draft reorganization plan;

(ii) The reorganization investor gives a presentation;

(iii) The administrator/the debtor and the reorganization investor answer creditors' inquiries concerning the draft reorganization plan; and

(iv) Each voting group cast ballots.

Article 244 Adjournment of vote

If a vote on a draft reorganization plan is impacted by force majeure or other objective obstacles occurred at a creditors' meeting, the voting may be adjourned with the permission of the People's Court, and the voting groups shall be notified of the time, place, voting method and other issues of the deferred vote.

Article 245 Creditors' vote

A draft reorganization plan shall be deemed adopted if approved by at least 50% creditors of the same voting group present at a creditors' meeting who account for at least 2/3 of the total claims of that group.

Article 246 Request for approval of a reorganization plan

A draft reorganization plan, if passed by all voting groups, shall be considered adopted.

The administrator, also the draft reorganization plan preparer, shall submit, within ten days from adoption thereof, an application for approval of the plan to the People's Court, accompanied by the reorganization plan and the voting result of each voting group.

Where the debtor requests the Court to rule on approval of a reorganization plan, the administrator shall comment on the legality of the voting.

Chapter V Reorganization

Article 247 Consultations and revote on a draft reorganization plan

If a draft reorganization plan fails to be adopted by a certain voting group, the administrator may consult with the group concerned and adjust the relevant contents thereof, provided that such adjustment shall not harm the interests of the creditors in other voting groups.

The voting groups disapproving the draft reorganization plan may revote, regardless of whether the relevant contents in the draft have been adjusted or not.

Article 248 Request for compulsory approval from the People's Court

If the voting group that fails to adopt a draft reorganization plan refuses to revote or the draft remains unadopted in a second vote, the administrator or the debtor shall timely report in writing to the People's Court.

The debtor or the administrator may apply to the Court for approval of a draft reorganization plan if it meets the following conditions:

(i) Under the draft, a secured claim against the debtor's property will be paid off in full with respect to the secured property, and the creditor will be fairly compensated for any losses incurred as a result of a delayed liquidation without substantive harm to the creditor's security interest; or the voting group concerned has adopted the draft;

(ii) Under the draft, the claims listed in Subparagraphs 2 & 3, Paragraph 1, Article 82 of the Enterprise Bankruptcy Law will be paid off in full, or the voting group concerned has adopted the draft;

(iii) Under the draft, the percentage of a general claim receiving payment shall not be lower than that under the bankruptcy liquidation procedure when the draft is submitted for approval, or the voting group concerned has adopted the draft;

(iv) The adjustment of the contributors' equity under the draft is fair and just, or the group of contributors has adopted the draft;

(v) The draft treats members of the same voting group equally, and the priority for repayment of claims thereunder is consistent with the provisions of Article 113 of the Enterprise Bankruptcy Law concerning the priority for repayment and pro rata payment of claims of the same priority; and

(vi) The debtor's business plan is feasible.

Article 249 Basic conditions for applying for compulsory approval

Where a draft reorganization plan is applied for compulsory approval, it shall be adopted through voting by at least one voting group whose rights and interests has been adjusted.

Article 250 Demonstration before application for compulsory approval

Before applying to the People's Court for compulsory approval, the administrator shall analyze the reasons behind the failure of adoption of a draft reorganization plan by a voting group, identify the opposing opinions one by one, and further demonstrate the legality, rationality and feasibility of the draft, as well as the key issues and legal risks inherent in its implementation, and expound on other matters like the preventive measures against such risks. The application submitted to the People's Court shall be generally accompanied with an analysis and demonstration report.

Article 251 Failed Adoption of a Draft Reorganization Plan

Where the debtor fails to submit a draft reorganization plan within the prescribed period, or the draft fails to be adopted and approved in accordance with Article 87 of the Enterprise Bankruptcy Law, the administrator shall file with the People's Court for a ruling to terminate the reorganization proceedings and declare the debtor bankrupt.

Article 252 Treatment of claims not filed within the filing period

There are circumstances where a creditor, who fails to submit claims within the period for filing, submits his claims later before a draft reorganization plan is submitted to a creditors' meeting for voting, which however have not been recognized. In that case, the creditor shall not be entitled to vote on the draft, unless he has been granted temporary voting rights by the People's Court.

There are also circumstances where a creditor, who fails to submit claims within the period for filing, files his claims later before the draft is submitted to a creditors' meeting for voting, which are later recognized by the People's Court. In that case, the recognized claims of the creditor may, upon the Court's approval, be paid off in accordance with the claim repayment scheme included the reorganization plan.

Section 7 Debt-for-Equity Swap

Article 253 Repayment with equity

As practically required by reorganization, claims against the debtor may, based on the voluntary principle, be satisfied by converting the debts to equity.

When a debt-for-equity swap scheme is provided in a draft reorganization plan, it is encouraged to also offer a cash repayment scheme, or a combination of two, as alternative options for creditors if conditions permit.

Article 254 Application of multiple means

The following ways may be employed to formulate a debt-for-equity swap scheme in accordance with the law:

(i) With respect to prohibition against commercial banks from holding equity investment in companies under the law on commercial banks, as well as other restrictions against certain subjects from equity investment, the debt-equity swap scheme may treat the enforcement body designated by the creditor concerned as the equity holder after the swap;

(ii) Catering to the varying needs of creditors accepting debt-equity swap, reorganization investors and original shareholders, new types of equity and swap ratio may be created legally. For example, the equity after the swap may be granted different ranks of priority, and the one held by original shareholders may be converted into shares based on a certain ratio; or

(iii) In view of the fact that the cash flow of a company may not be substantively changed after the debt-equity swap, financing approaches for the debtor may be diversified on the basis of the traditional ones, which suggests debt-equity swap may be used in conjunction with other financing approaches such as issuing convertible bonds and equity investment products.

Article 255 Debt-equity swap and asset restructuring

In the formulation and implementation process of the debt-equity swap scheme, assets may be restructured through revitalization, purchase, sale of assets or other means which may inspire positive changes in the debtor, especially its business, assets and income. Additionally, debt-equity swap may be effectively linked up with asset restructuring and carried out simultaneously with the latter, which may raise the debt repayment percentage and the continuous profitability growth of the debtor after reorganization.

Article 256 Reconversion mechanism

The debt-equity swap scheme may provide for a mechanism for reconverting equity to debts in case of failure of a reorganization plan. Eligible creditors accepting debt-equity swap may opt out of shareholder rights and reconvert equity into debts; and the claims in question may be discharged in the order of priority determined before the debt-equity swap. The fundamental reconversion mechanism covers:

(i) When creditors accepting debt-equity swap opt out of shareholder rights in case of failure of a reorganization plan, the commitment made by such creditors with respect to the debt-equity swap and adjustment of claims shall be invalidated according to the Enterprise Bankruptcy Law, Article 93, Paragraph 2, and the equity may be reconverted into debts;

(ii) Where the equity held by a creditor is reconverted into debts, any additional repayment or distribution shall also be made to the creditor after he is paid off under the same conditions as other creditors enjoying the same rank of priority but not having swapped debts for equity.

Article 257 Vote on and effectiveness of a debt-equity swap scheme

The provisions on voting and approval of a draft reorganization plan shall also apply to a debt-equity swap scheme, as the latter is an integral part of the former.

Section 8 Implementation of a Reorganization Plan

Article 258 Subjects responsible for implementing a reorganization plan

If the People's Court approves a reorganization plan, the debtor shall be responsible for the implementation thereof.

Article 259 Handover of assets and business affairs

Upon the People's Court approval of a reorganization plan, the administrator responsible for management of a debtor's assets and business affairs shall hand over such assets and affairs to the debtor in a timely manner.

Article 260 Binding force of a reorganization plan

A reorganization plan approved by the People's Court is binding on the debtor and all creditors. It is also binding on all the contributors of the debtor, if adjustment of contributors' equity is contemplated therein.

The rights of a creditor against any guarantor of the debtor and any other joint debtor shall neither be affected by the reorganization plan, nor by the voting results of the creditor thereon.

The debtor shall, as of completion of implementation of a reorganization plan, no longer be liable for repayment of any debts forgiven pursuant thereto.

Article 261 Treatment of restrictions on original equity

If a debtor is insolvent and the equity subject to adjustment under a reorganization plan has been pledged as collateral, the administrator may coordinate with the pledgee to go through the procedures to cancel the pledge.

Chapter V Reorganization

Article 262 Modification of contributors' equity and its execution

When adjustment of contributors' equity is contemplated in a reorganization plan, the administrator shall supervise the contributors concerned to register the changes to equity.

The administrator or the debtor may apply to the Court to issue a notice for assistance in execution to the relevant entities and then handle the equity transfer procedures by taking compulsory execution measures, if the contributor concerned refuses to cooperate in handling such procedures when the equity subject to adjustment under a reorganization plan is not pledged but frozen, or is neither pledged nor frozen.

Article 263 Supervision on implementation of a reorganization plan

Upon the Court approval of a reorganization plan, the administrator shall supervise its implementation according to its own provisions. He shall also participate in pending actions or arbitration, if any, on behalf of the debtor during the execution of the plan.

The administrator shall devise a supervision scheme where supervision methods, matters subject to supervision and supervisory duties are specified. He shall also urge the debtor to fully implement the reorganization plan within the execution period.

The execution period of a reorganization plan shall, in principle, be consistent with its supervision period. In case of any conflict, the remuneration scheme for the administrator under the reorganization proceedings shall be determined and adjusted in line with his different workload during the two periods. Specifically, his remuneration during the execution period may be determined and paid by considering the actual role he has played in reorganization and other factors; and the payment percentage and time of his remuneration during the supervision period may, based on his performance of supervisory duties, be compliant with the actual repayment percentage and time for creditors under the reorganization plan.

Article 264 Duties of the administrator during the period of supervision of the implementation of a reorganization plan

The administrator shall perform supervisory duties during the supervision period stipulated in a reorganization plan, which primarily include:

(i) To formulate a supervision scheme, specifying reporting items and time for the debtor and supervision methods and matters subject to supervision for the administrator, and then submit the scheme to the People's Court;

(ii) To require the debtor to report the implementation of a reorganization plan and its asset status according to the supervision scheme;

(iii) To promptly rectify the debtor's offense or other improper behaviors, if any;

(iv) To apply to the People's Court for an extension of the supervision period when necessary; and

(v) To submit a supervision report to the People's Court at the expiry of the supervision period.

Article 265 The administrator's supervision on the debtor

The administrator shall, during the period of supervision, require the debtor to timely report in writing to himself on implementation of a reorganization plan and its asset status, and then timely report to the People's Court.

The administrator may require the debtor to transfer the funds for debt repayment under the reorganization plan approved by the Court to the account of the administrator, who shall make or supervise the repayment.

Article 266 Supervision report

At the expiration of the period of supervision of the implementation of a reorganization plan, the administrator shall submit a supervision report on its implementation to the People's Court. The report shall reflect the debtor's implementation of the plan and the implementation effects. The administrator shall, upon application by any stakeholder under the plan, provide the supervision report to the person for reference.

Article 267 Extension of implementation and supervision periods

Where the debtor applies for an extension of the implementation period of a reorganization plan, the administrator shall inspect the same and submit his supervisory opinions to the People's Court, which shall cover the actual implementation progress, the reasons for the failure to fully implement the plan as scheduled, and the feasibility of the debtor's work plan for the next stage. The administrator shall file with the Court for a ruling to extend the implementation and supervision periods prior to their expiry if such extension is considered necessary.

Article 268 Modification during the implementation of a reorganization plan

The administrator shall supervise the debtor to strictly implement a reorganization plan. However, if the plan cannot be implemented due to special circumstances such as adjustment of national policies or amendment of laws, the administrator may propose to hold a creditors' meeting to vote on the modification of the plan.

If a creditors' meeting passes a resolution to modify the reorganization plan, the administrator shall, within ten days from the date of adoption of the resolution, submit a written report to the People's Court, accompanied by the voting results, requesting the latter for approval. In the event of failure to pass such a resolution or the People's Court disapproval over the application for modification, the administrator shall submit a written report to the Court, accompanied with relevant materials, requesting the latter to order to terminate the implementation of the plan and declare the debtor bankrupt.

Article 269 Voting and approval of a modified reorganization plan

Where the modification of a reorganization plan gets approved by the People's Court, the debtor or the administrator shall offer a new modified plan within six months, which shall only be submitted to the group of creditors or contributors adversely affected for voting. During this period, the administrator shall perform his duties with reference to those in the reorganization period.

Article 270 Completion of implementation of a reorganization plan

Upon completion of the implementation of a reorganization plan, the administrator may apply to the People's Court for an order confirming the same and terminating the bankruptcy proceedings.

Article 271 Termination of the administrator's duties

The supervisory duties of the administrator shall terminate from the submission date of the supervision report.

Section 9 Termination of Reorganization Proceedings

Article 272 Termination of a reorganization plan implementation

If the debtor is unable or fails to implement a reorganization plan, the administrator shall timely submit a written report to the People's Court, accompanied with relevant materials, requesting the latter to order to terminate the implementation of the plan and declare the debtor bankrupt.

Article 273 Application for termination of reorganization proceeding

The administrator shall timely prepare a report and submit it to the People's Court, requesting the latter to rule to terminate the reorganization proceedings and declare the debtor bankrupt, if any of the following circumstances occurs in the process of reorganization.

(i) Reorganization of the debtor becomes a nullity or the debtor is unable to be rescued due to the continuous deterioration of its business and assets, as well as other reasons;

(ii) The debtor commits fraud, maliciously reduces its assets, or engages in any other practice obviously detrimental to creditors;

(iii) The act of the debtor prevents the administrator from performing his duties;

(iv) A draft reorganization plan fails to be in place within the statutory time limit; and

(v) The reorganization plan is disapproved by the People's Court.

The report shall detail the situation which renders the continuing of the reorganization proceedings a nullity. If the business and asset conditions of the debtor under reorganization continue to worsen, the report shall also indicate the extent of deterioration, accompanied by relevant documentation.

Article 274 Conversion from reorganization proceedings to bankruptcy liquidation

After the Court issues an order to terminate the reorganization proceedings and declares the debtor bankrupt, the administrator shall perform his duties in accordance with the bankruptcy liquidation procedure if he is responsible for management of the debtor's assets and business affairs. Where the management of such assets and affairs is in the charge of the debtor itself, the administrator shall immediately take over the debtor's seals, account books and assets, and conduct bankruptcy liquidation of the debtor in accordance with the relevant provisions of the Enterprise Bankruptcy Law.

Chapter VI Pre-reorganization

Section 1 General Provisions

Article 275 Pre-reorganization period

The pre-reorganization period commences from the date when the People's Court decides to pre-reorganize to the date when the Court rules to accept or dismiss a reorganization application, or allows the withdrawal of such an application.

Article 276 Appointment of an administrator for pre-reorganization

In the process of pre-reorganization, an administrator therefor may be recommended by the debtor and major creditors through consultation. Candidates of administrator shall be selected from the list of bankruptcy administrators prepared by Guangdong Higher People's Court.

Section 2   Duties of the Administrator for Pre-reorganization

Article 277 Duties of the administrator for pre-reorganization

Duties of the administrator for pre-reorganization may include:

(i) To fully investigate into the debtor's basic situation, assets and liabilities, as well as involvement in actions, arbitration or enforcement, and then prepare a report on the assets of the debtor;

(ii) To issue an announcement of registration of claims to verify the debtor's liabilities;

(iii) To supervise the debtor's property safekeeping and business operation, whether the debtor has violated its pre-reorganization commitment, evaded or abolished debts, repaid debts selectively, or committed any other act devaluing its property to the detriment of creditors; and to timely report the same to the People's Court;

(iv) To call for meetings of creditors, investors and debtors;

(v) To coordinate to suspend execution;

(vi) To apply to the People's Court for measures to preserve or realize all or part of the debtor's assets when such assets are possibly losing their value;

(vii) To collect information about whether any known creditor or public citizen is interested in the debtor's reorganization and composition, and to recruit prospective investors for reorganization;

(viii) To urge the debtor to draft a pre-reorganization plan through consultation with contributors, creditors, prospective reorganization investors and other interested parties;

(ix) To timely acquire crucial information related to the debtor's application for reorganization, regularly and timely report the administrator's work progress to the People's Court in writing, and cooperate with the debtor to objectively and thoroughly explain and clarify some relevant issues of public concern;

(x) To examine whether the debtor has reorganization value and reorganization feasibility grounds;

(xi) To submit a work report on pre-reorganization to the People's Court, apply for an extension of the pre-reorganization period or the termination of the pre-reorganization procedure based on the inspection results; and

(xii) Other duties required by the People's Court to be performed by the pre-reorganization administrator.

Article 278 The debtor's obligations

During the pre-reorganization period, the administrator may supervise and urge the debtor to perform the following obligations:

(i) To properly keep its assets, seals, account books, documents and other materials;

(ii) To cooperate with the pre-reorganization administrator to get investigation, audit, evaluation work done by truthfully answering relevant inquiries and submitting pertinent documents;

(iii) To diligently operate its business and properly maintain the value of its enterprise assets;

(iv) To truthfully disclose information concerning any hypothecation, pledge or guaranty on its property, assets preservation, external guarantee and other contingent debts;

(v) To timely report to the pre-reorganization administrator any act and matter that have a major impact on its assets, and subject to the administrator's supervision;

(vi) To truthfully disclose information related to pre-reorganization to contributors, creditors, prospective investors and other interested parties, and to explain the draft pre-reorganization plan and answer relevant inquiries;

(vii) Not to discharge external debts, except for expenditures necessary for its continued operation and the maintenance of its operating value;

(viii) Not to provide guarantee for any third party without the consent of the Peoples' Court;

(ix) To work out a draft pre-reorganization plan upon active consultation with contributors, creditors, prospective reorganization investors and other interested parties;

(x) Where the debtor signs a new contract, continues to perform an executory contract or carries out any other major act involving disposition of assets, business operation and appointment or removal of employees, it shall report to the pre-reorganization administrator before making a decision, and subject to the supervision of the latter.

(xi) To complete other tasks in connection with pre-reorganization.

Article 279 Disclosure of information

The pre-reorganization administrator shall require the debtor to comprehensively, accurately, and legally disclose any and all information related to reorganization to creditors, contributors, reorganization investors and other interested parties.

The information that the debtor is required to disclose include: (a) causes of reorganization, (b) its production, operation and financial conditions, (c) its contract performance capability, (d) its assets status, and details of its liabilities such as external guarantee and contingent debts, (e) its involvement in actions, arbitration or enforcement, particularly significant and uncertain actions or arbitration, (f) repayment rate in a simulated bankruptcy liquidation, (g) investment plan of any prospective reorganization investor, and (h) the major risks underlying a draft pre-reorganization plan.

Article 280 Hiring a professional organization

The pre-reorganization administrator may, upon approval of the Court, engage professional organizations like auditing and evaluation firms in accordance with the Enterprise Bankruptcy Law.

Article 281 Borrowings during pre-reorganization

During the reorganization period, if the debtor needs to take out loans for continuing business, the pre-reorganization administrator shall comment on the debtor's loan application upon examination and report to the Court.

Article 282 Notice to creditors

The pre-reorganization administrator shall notify the known creditors in writing to file their claims. The contents of the notice shall include:

(i) The date when the Court decides the debtor's pre-reorganization;

(ii) Time limit for filing;

(iii) Name, contact person and contact information of the pre-reorganization administrator;

(iv) The data required for filing a claim, including the basic information of a creditor, how a debt forms, amount of the original debt principal, amount of the yield up to the date of pre-reorganization, method to calculate yield, a list of interest and the amount of debt calculated, whether the claim is secured by property, whether it is a joint claim, and the debt maturity date, accompanied with relevant evidence; and

(v) Other matters required to be notified by the Court or the pre-reorganization administrator.

Section 3 Preparation and Adoption of a Draft Pre-reorganization Plan

Article 283 Preparation and adoption of a draft pre-reorganization plan

The pre-reorganization administrator shall supervise and urge the debtor to draw up a draft pre-reorganization plan, taking into account opinions of contributors, creditors, prospective investors and other interested parties, which are collected upon communication with them on the premise of full disclosure of information.

The draft pre-reorganization plan shall include the details under Article 81 of the Enterprise Bankruptcy Law.

In line with Articles 82, 84, 85 and 86 of the Enterprise Bankruptcy Law, the pre-reorganization plan shall be formed after approval by creditors, contributors and other interested parties through voting.

Article 284 Disclosure of information on adjustment of contributors' equity

If a draft pre-reorganization plan involves adjustment of contributors' equity, the contributors concerned shall be obliged to truthfully disclose any action, arbitration and enforcement involving their equity, and the debtor and its contributors shall truthfully disclose any pledge, preservation or any other encumbrance created on contributors' equity.

Section 4 Termination of Pre-reorganization

Article 285 Application for termination of pre-reorganization

During the pre-reorganization period, if the debtor is under any of the following circumstances, the pre-reorganization administrator shall timely file an application with the People's Court for termination of the pre-reorganization proceedings, which shall indicate the facts and grounds on which the application is based.

(i) Reorganization investors have been recruited as expected and a pre-reorganization plan is in place, and the pre-reorganization administrator recommends the reorganization application be accepted;

(ii) The debtor has no reason for reorganization;

(iii) The debtor has no reorganization value;

(iv) It is impossible for the debtor to be reorganized;

(v) Certain crucial property of the debtor is about to be disposed of or the disposal price is about to be realized, which may cause serious damages to the debtor's reorganization value if the reorganization application is not accepted;

(vi) The debtor is under any of the circumstances prescribed in Articles 31, 32 and 33 of the Enterprise Bankruptcy Law, or other circumstances that may seriously harm the interests of creditors;

(vii) The debtor refuses to perform its obligations hereunder, resulting in the failure to serve the purpose of pre-reorganization;

(viii) The debtor is neither able to pay the necessary pre-reorganization expenses itself, nor have such expenses paid by others;

(ix) The applicant has withdrawn his pre-reorganization application from the People's Court;

(x) Other circumstances where the pre-reorganization proceedings shall be terminated.

Article 286 Submission of report

Upon completion of pre-reorganization or expiration of the pre-reorganization period, the pre-reorganization administrator shall submit a work report thereon to the People's Court.

Such a report shall generally include:

(i) Basic information of the debtor;

(ii) Causes for the debtor's operational or financial difficulties;

(iii) The debtor's assets and liabilities;

(iv) The debtor's production and operation status;

(v) Analysis and comments on the value of the debtor's reorganization;

(vi) Analysis and comments on the feasibility of the debtor's reorganization;

(vii) Whether a pre-reorganization plan has been formed and the negotiation thereon, or alternatively the reasons why the said plan fails;

(viii) Potential risks of reorganization and relevant recommendations;

(ix) The major work already completed by the pre-reorganization administrator;

(x) Whether to apply for entering the reorganization proceedings;

(xi) Other circumstances that should be reported.

Chapter VI Pre-reorganization

Section 5 Connection of Pre-reorganization and Reorganization Procedures

Article 287 Connection between the pre-reorganization plan and the draft reorganization plan

Before accepting the reorganization application, if the debtor formulates a pre-reorganization plan or reaches a pre-reorganization agreement through out-of-court commercial negotiations, it shall disclose information and collect creditors, capital contributors, investors of the pre-reorganization party and other stakeholders' comments in accordance with the provisions of The Operational Guidelines.

The pre-reorganization plan shall include the main contents stipulated in Article 81 of the Enterprise Bankruptcy Law. After the reorganization application is accepted, the debtor or the administrator may make and submit a draft reorganization plan based on the pre-reorganization plan.

During the pre-reorganization period, the creditor's rights adjustment, debt repayment, investor's rights adjustment, etc., the agreement reached between the creditor, the investor and the debtor, and the creditor's and investor's consent to the pre-reorganization plan, if any of the following conditions are met, continue to be valid after the reorganization application is accepted:

(i) The basic content of the draft reorganization plan is consistent with the content of the relevant agreement or the commitment and consent of creditors and investors, or an arrangement more beneficial to the interests of creditors or investors is made;

(ii) The modification of the draft reorganization plan to the relevant agreement or the commitment and consent of creditors and investors does not substantially affect the interests of the creditors and investors, and the relevant creditors and investors agree to no longer vote on the draft reorganization plan.

Article 288 Connection of claims filing

The creditors who have submitted the creditor's claims filing materials to the pre-reorganization administrator during the pre-reorganization stage shall be deemed to have declared the creditor's rights after officially entering the reorganization procedure, and there is no need to repeat filing.

Article 289 Recommended application for transfer-in reorganization

The pre-reorganization administrator may, according to the work situation of the pre-reorganization, propose to the court to apply for a transfer to the reorganization procedure. If the debtor, creditor or pre-reorganization administrator applies for transferring into the reorganization procedure, it shall submit to the People's Court a pre-reorganization work report, a written application for transferring into the reorganization, the pre-reorganization plan, and the creditors, capital contributors and other stakeholders' comments on the reorganization plan, etc.

Article 290 Administrator connection

For a case that has entered the reorganization procedure after pre-reorganization, the debtor, creditor, investor and other stakeholders, as well as the pre-reorganization administrator, may request the People's Court to designate the pre-reorganization administrator as the administrator of the reorganization case.

The work completed by the pre-reorganization administrator during the pre-reorganization process may be inherited by the administrator after examination during the reorganization process.

Section 6 Pre-reorganization Administrator Remuneration and Pre-reorganization Expenses

Article 291 Remuneration of pre-reorganization administrators

The remuneration of the pre-reorganization administrator shall be determined in accordance with the provisions of the Supreme People's Court on Determining the Remuneration of the Administrator in the Trial of Enterprise Bankruptcy Cases, and comprehensively determined based on the actual performance of duties and effects of the pre-reorganization administrator during the pre-reorganization period.

If the People's Court decides to re-designate the administrator when accepting the reorganization application, during the pre-reorganization period, if the pre-reorganization administrator has made reasonable labor for the introduction of investors, the negotiation, preparation of the pre-reorganization plan, and the collection of opinions, the amount of remuneration may be negotiated between the pre-reorganization administrator and the debtor. If negotiation fails, it shall be decided by the People's Court.

After the end of the pre-reorganization procedure, if the People's Court rules to allow the applicant to withdraw the application for reorganization, the work remuneration of the pre-reorganization administrator shall be determined according to the prior or subsequent negotiation between the pre-reorganization administrator and the pre-reorganization participants. If negotiation fails, it shall be reported to the People's Court for decision.

Article 292 Pre-reorganization fee

During the pre-reorganization period, the pre-reorganization manager's fees and remuneration for performing duties, audit evaluation, professional consultation and other pre-reorganization expenses shall be determined through negotiation between each professional institution and the pre-reorganization participants, and shall be implemented in accordance with the agreement.

After the People's Court has ruled to accept the reorganization application, the pre-reorganization expenses that the debtor has not paid may be handled as bankruptcy expenses.

Chapter VII Composition

Section 1 General Provisions

Article 293 Office term of the administrator during the composition procedure

The period during which the administrator performs its duties in the composition procedure starts from the time the People's Court decides composition procedure and ends when the Court decides to terminate the composition procedure.

Article 294 Duties of the administrator

If the People's Court decides composition, the administrator shall perform the administrator's duties in accordance with the legal provisions and The Operational Guidelines, unless the creditors' meeting has resolved otherwise and does not violate the legal provisions.

Section 2 Initiation of Composition Proceedings

Article 295 Guiding the debtor to apply for composition

If the debtor has the intention of composition, the administrator shall inform the debtor to apply to the People's Court for composition before the bankruptcy declaration, and submit a draft composition agreement at the same time.

Article 296 Preparation of a draft composition agreement

The administrator may assist the debtor in formulating or revising the draft composition agreement, and submit a written report to the creditors' meeting, stating the legitimacy and feasibility of the draft, for consideration by the creditors' meeting.

The draft composition agreement generally includes the following contents.

(i) The property status of the debtor;

(ii) The proportion, time limit and source of property for repayment of debts;

(iii) Bankruptcy expenses, type, amount and payment time limit of common debts.

The debtor can set security clauses for the execution of the composition agreement in the draft composition agreement; it can also formulate supervision clauses and set up a supervisor for the execution of the composition agreement.

Article 297 Notice to convene a meeting of creditors

After the People's Court makes a ruling on composition, the administrator may assist the Court to notify the creditors' meeting to discuss the draft composition agreement.

Chapter VII Composition

Article 298 Composition agreement voted at the creditors' meeting

The resolution of the composition agreement adopted by the creditors' meeting shall be approved by more than half of the creditors with voting rights present at the meeting, and the amount of creditor's rights represented by them shall account for more than two-thirds of the total unsecured creditor's rights.

Article 299 Processing after the composition agreement is passed

If the composition agreement is approved by the creditors' meeting, the administrator shall promptly apply to the People's Court for a ruling to approve the composition agreement, terminate the composition procedure, and make an announcement after the creditors' meeting. After the People's Court makes a ruling, the administrator shall hand over the property and business affairs to the debtor, and submit a duty performance report to the People's Court.

Article 300 After the composition agreement is not approved

If the draft composition agreement has not been approved by the creditors' meeting, or the composition agreement that has been passed at the creditors' meeting has not been approved by the People's Court, the administrator shall promptly apply to the People's Court for a ruling to terminate the composition procedure and declare the debtor bankrupt.

Section 3 Implementation of the Composition Proceedings

Article 301 Supervising the implementation of the composition agreement

The administrator can assist the composition creditors in monitoring the implementation of the composition agreement.

Article 302 Secured party exercising security right

The obligee who enjoys the security right in the specific property of the debtor may claim to the administrator to exercise the security right from the date when the People's Court decides composition.

Article 303 Restrictions on equity transfer of debtor's shareholders

After the composition is ruled, without the permission of the People's Court, the administrator shall not assist the debtor's shareholder in handling the equity transfer procedures.

Article 304 Unfiled claims

After the implementation of composition agreement is completed, the composition creditors who have not filed their claims may exercise their rights in accordance with the repayment conditions stipulated in the composition agreement.

Article 305 Ways to Implement of Composition Agreement

If the People's Court has ruled to recognize the composition agreement and terminate the composition procedure, the administrator may require the debtor to transfer the funds used for debt repayment into the administrator's account for unified payment in accordance with the provisions of the composition agreement.

Chapter VII Composition

Article 306 Handover obligation and work report

If the People's Court decides to approve the composition agreement and terminate the composition procedure, the administrator shall hand over the property and business affairs to the debtor, write an explanation of the changes in the debtor's property and business affairs during the period when the administrator takes over, and submit a report on the execution of duties to the People's Court.

The report shall list the duties performed by the administrator in such aspects as work preparation, property takeover, clearing of creditor's rights and debts, filing and registration of creditor's claims, etc., after the administrator accepts the appoitment. The report also shall focus on report the adoption of the composition agreement and the transfer of property and business affairs.

Article 307 Completion of the implementation of composition agreement and termination of the composition procedure

After the implementation of the composition agreement is completed, the administrator shall promptly submit a report on the termination of duties to the People's Court, and apply to the Court for a ruling to terminate the bankruptcy procedure.

Section 4 Termination of Composition Proceedings

Article 308 The composition agreement is invalid

If the administrator finds that the composition agreement is established due to the debtor's fraud or other illegal acts, it shall promptly submit a written report to the People's Court, request the Court to rule that the composition agreement is invalid, and declare the debtor bankrupt.

Article 309 The composition agreement cannot be enforced

If the debtor is unable to implement or does not implement the composition agreement, the administrator may seek the opinion of the composition creditor, and within 15 days after the composition creditors agree, apply to the People's Court for a ruling to terminate the execution of the composition agreement and declare the debtor bankrupt.

If the People's Court terminates the execution of the composition agreement, the composition creditor's commitment to adjust the creditor's rights in the composition agreement shall be invalid. The repayment of the composition creditor due to the execution of the composition agreement is still valid, and the unpaid part of the composition creditor's right is regarded as the bankruptcy creditor's right. However, the creditor can continue to accept the distribution only when other creditors in the same order have received the same proportion of the repayment. The guarantees provided for the enforcement of the composition agreement remain in effect.

Article 310 Handling of self-composition

After the People's Court accepts the bankruptcy application, if the debtor and all creditors reach an agreement on the handling of the debtor and creditor's rights and debts, the administrator may request the People's Court to approve and terminate the bankruptcy procedure.

If the People's Court decides to approve the composition agreement reached by the debtor and all creditors on its own and terminate the bankruptcy procedure, the administrator shall hand over the property and business affairs to the debtor, write an explanation of the changes in the debtor's property and business affairs during the period when the administrator takes over, and submit a report on performance of duties to the People's Court at the same time.

Section 5 Handling of Failed Composition

Article 311 Handling of failed composition

Under any of the following circumstances, the administrator shall take over the debtor's property and business affairs in a timely manner, and perform its duties in accordance with the bankruptcy liquidation procedure.

(i) If the draft composition agreement has not been approved by the creditors' meeting, or the composition agreement that has been adopted at the creditors' meeting has not been approved by the People's Court, the Court rules to terminate the composition procedure and declare the debtor bankrupt;

(ii) The People's Court rules that the composition agreement is invalid and declares the debtor bankrupt;

(iii) The People's Court rules to terminate the implementation of the composition agreement and declares the debtor bankrupt.

Chapter VIII   Cross-border Insolvency

Section 1   Guidelines for Mainland Work of Hong Kong Managers

Article 312 Definition

The "overseas insolvency proceedings" mentioned in The Operational Guidelines refers to the collective repayment proceedings in accordance with the Hong Kong bankruptcy laws and regulations stipulated by "Minutes of the Meeting between the Supreme People's Court and the Government of the Hong Kong Special Administrative Region on Mutual Recognition and Assistance in Bankruptcy Proceedings by the Courts of Mainland and the Hong Kong Special Administrative Region" and "Opinions of the Supreme People's Court on Launching the Pilot Work of Recognizing and Assisting the Bankruptcy Procedures in the Hong Kong Special Administrative Region".

The "Hong Kong administrator" referred to in The Operational Guidelines includes liquidators and provisional liquidators in insolvency proceedings in Hong Kong.

Article 313 Scope of application

The overseas insolvency proceedings to which The Operational Guidelines apply are Hong Kong insolvency proceedings in which the debtor's center of main interests is located in the Hong Kong Special Administrative Region.

The "center of main interests" as mentioned in These Operational Guidelines generally refers to the place of registration of the debtor. At the same time, the People's Court shall comprehensively consider factors such as the location of the debtor's main office, main business location, and main property location.

When the Hong Kong administrator applies for recognition and assistance, the debtor's center of main interests should have existed in Hong Kong for more than 6 consecutive months.

Article 314 Ways to perform duties by Hong Kong administrators

Hong Kong administrators may perform their duties in Mainland in two ways: in person or by entrusting others to perform their duties.

If a Hong Kong administrator performs his duties in Mainland in person, the scope of his duties shall not exceed the provisions of the Enterprise Bankruptcy Law or the provisions of Hong Kong law.

If a Hong Kong manager entrusts a Mainland manager to perform duties, the client and the trustee shall negotiate and determine their respective rights, obligations, and scope of responsibility, and the client shall clearly explain to the trustee in advance the procedural and substantive relevant provisions of the matters to be entrusted. Both parties need to sign a formal written entrustment contract, and provide Chinese or Chinese and English versions. Before signing the entrustment contract, the Hong Kong administrator shall report the matters to be signed and the text of the entrustment contract to the People's Court hearing cross-border insolvency cases.

Article 315 The Hong Kong administrator entrusts Mainland administrator

If the Hong Kong administrator needs to entrust Mainland administrator to handle matters related to the application for recognition and assistance in overseas insolvency proceedings, it may adopt the method of entrusting as a whole or entrusting individual matters.

Overall entrustment refers to the manner in which the Hong Kong administrator entrusts the same trustee with all relevant matters within Mainland for requesting recognition and assistance in overseas insolvency proceedings. For details of the entrustment, please refer to Article 322 of the "The Scope of Administrator's Responsibilities" of these business operation guidelines.

Entrustment of individual matters refers to the manner in which the Hong Kong administrator individually appoints a trustee for matters related to the application for recognition and assistance in overseas insolvency proceedings.

Article 316 Circumstances of not accepting entrustment

Upon review, if the Hong Kong bankruptcy procedure for which the client applies for recognition and assistance falls under any of the following circumstances, the trustee shall not accept the entrustment:

(i) As of the date when the Hong Kong administrator applies for recognition and assistance in bankruptcy proceedings in Hong Kong, the debtor's center of main interests is not in Hong Kong;

(ii) As of the date when the Hong Kong administrator files an application for recognition and assistance in bankruptcy proceedings in Hong Kong, the debtor's center of main interests is in Hong Kong, but the period of continuous residence in Hong Kong is less than six months;

(iii) Mainland People's Court has initiated bankruptcy proceedings against the same debtor;

(iv) The Hong Kong administrator in the Hong Kong bankruptcy proceedings has a situation that damages the legitimate rights and interests of Mainland creditors to participate in the Hong Kong bankruptcy proceedings on an equal basis, and fails to propose remedial measures;

(v) The debtor does not have the bankruptcy reasons specified in Article 2 of the Enterprise Bankruptcy Law;

(vi) There is fraud;

(vii) Recognizing or assisting the insolvency proceedings in Hong Kong violates the basic principles of Mainland laws or violates public order and public morals;

(viii) Other circumstances in which the People's Court deems that recognition or assistance should not be granted.

If the bankruptcy proceedings in Hong Kong that have been approved and assisted by the client have the above circumstances, the client shall be required to make statements, explanations and supplementary materials. If there is no such circumstance after review, the entrustment shall be accepted in accordance with these business operation guidelines. If the above-mentioned circumstances exist after review, the reason shall be explained to the client and the client shall refuse to accept the entrustment.

Article 317　Apply to a court of competent jurisdiction

If the debtor's main property is located in the pilot area of Mainland, has a place of business in the pilot area of Mainland, or has a representative office in the pilot area of Mainland, the Hong Kong administrator may apply for recognition and assistance in insolvency proceedings commenced in Hong Kong.

Cross-border insolvency cases shall be under the jurisdiction of the intermediate People's Court in the pilot area where the main property, business place or representative office is located. If the Hong Kong administrator applies to two or more People's Courts with jurisdiction at the same time, he shall notify the People's Court reviewing the case of the situation under which other Court has already accepted the case.

Article 318　Materials for application for recognition and assistance in overseas insolvency proceedings

To apply for recognition and assistance in overseas insolvency proceedings, a Hong Kong administrator shall submit the following materials.

(i) Application;

(ii) Letters from overseas courts requesting recognition and assistance;

(iii) Relevant documents on the opening of overseas proceedings, the appointment of a Hong Kong administrator and the scope of duties;

(iv) Evidence that the debtor's center of main interests is located outside Mainland, and if the material is formed outside the Mainland, the certification procedures shall also be completed in accordance with the provisions of Mainland laws;

(v) A copy of the judgment document applying for recognition and assistance;

(vi) Photocopies of the identity documents of the Hong Kong administrator and his/her contact person, if they were formed overseas, the certification procedures shall also be completed in accordance with the provisions of Mainland laws;

(vii) Relevant evidence that the debtor's main property is located in Mainland, has a place of business in Mainland, or has a representative office in Mainland;

(viii) Laws and regulations applicable to overseas insolvency proceedings.

If the documents submitted to the People's Court hearing cross-border bankruptcy assistance cases do not have Chinese versions, the Chinese translations and their certification documents shall be submitted.

Article 319 Items specified in the application form

The application form should state the following:

(i) The debtor's name, place of registration, and the name, position, domicile, identity document information, communication method, etc. of the debtor's main responsible person known to the Hong Kong administrator;

(ii) The name, domicile, identity document information, communication method, etc. of the administrator in Hong Kong;

(iii) The progress and plans of overseas insolvency proceedings;

(iv) Matters and reasons for applying for recognition and assistance;

(v) Information about the debtor's known property, place of business, representative office and creditors in Mainland;

(vi) Litigation and arbitration involving the debtor in Mainland, as well as the preservation measures and enforcement procedures of the debtor's property;

(vii) Relevant information on bankruptcy proceedings against the debtor in other countries or regions;

(viii) Other matters that should be specified.

Article 320 Interim relief before recognizing overseas insolvency proceedings

After the People's Court receives the application for recognition and assistance, but before making a ruling, the Hong Kong administrator may apply to the People's Court for preservation, requesting the People's Court to handle it in accordance with the relevant Mainland laws.

Article 321 Ruling to recognize the identity of Hong Kong administrator and announcement

The identity of the Hong Kong administrator, when the People's Court decides to approve the overseas insolvency proceedings, shall decide to approve it at the same time according to the application, and announce it within five days.

Article 322 Duties of the administrator

After the People's Court has ruled to recognize the overseas bankruptcy procedure, and at the same time has ruled to recognize its Hong Kong administrator status according to the application, the Hong Kong administrator can perform the following duties in Mainland:

(i) Taking over the debtor's property, seal, account books, documents and other materials;

(ii) Investigate the debtor's property status and prepare a property status report;

(iii) To decide on the internal management affairs of the debtor;

(iv) To decide the daily expenses and other necessary expenses of the debtor;

(v) before the first meeting of creditors, decide to continue or stop the debtor's business;

(vi) Manage and dispose of the debtor's property;

(vii) Participating in litigation, arbitration or other legal proceedings on behalf of the debtor;

(viii) Accepting and reviewing claims submitted by mainland creditors;

(ix) Other duties that the People's Court deems that the Hong Kong administrator may be allowed to perform.

When the Hong Kong administrator performs the duties as prescribed in the preceding paragraph, if it involves giving up property rights, setting property guarantees, borrowing money, transferring property out of Mainland, and implementing other property dispositions that have a significant impact on the interests of creditors, separate approval from the People's Court is required.

The performance of duties by the Hong Kong administrator shall not exceed the scope stipulated by the Enterprise Bankruptcy Law, nor the scope stipulated by the Hong Kong insolvency law.

Article 323 Appointment of Mainland Administrator

After the People's Court recognizes the overseas insolvency proceeding, the Hong Kong administrator or creditor may apply to the People's Court for the appointment of a Mainland administrator in the administrator list compiled by the Guangdong Higher People's Court.

After Mainland administrator is appointed, the duties of the Hong Kong administrator in Mainland shall be exercised by Mainland administrator, and the affairs and property of the debtor in Mainland shall be handled by the Enterprise Bankruptcy Law.

The administrators of the two jurisdictions should strengthen communication and cooperation.

Article 324 Change, termination of recognition and assistance

If any circumstance affecting the recognition and assistance of Hong Kong insolvency proceedings is discovered, the administrator shall promptly report to the People's Court and submit relevant materials so that the Court can change or terminate the recognition and assistance in a timely manner.

Article 325 Replacement of administrator

If the Hong Kong administrator is replaced, the original Hong Kong administrator and the new Hong Kong administrator shall report to the People's Court in a timely manner, and apply for the Court's ruling to recognize the identity of the new Hong Kong administrator.

The Hong Kong administrator may apply to the People's Court for the replacement of Mainland administrator with justifiable reasons.

Article 326 Cooperation between domestic and foreign administrators

Where Hong Kong and Mainland conduct separate insolvency proceedings for the same debtor or related debtors, the administrators of the two jurisdictions shall strengthen communication and cooperation.

Article 327 Assistance of Hong Kong administrator

The Hong Kong administrator shall assist in the communication and cooperation between the People's Court of Mainland, the Mainland creditors and the courts of Hong Kong and Hong Kong creditors.

Article 328 Principles of repayment to Hong Kong creditors

If the People's Court recognizes and assists the insolvency proceedings in Hong Kong, after the debtor's bankruptcy property in Mainland has paid off the debts that should be paid off in priority in accordance with the laws of Mainland, the remaining property shall be distributed and paid off in accordance with the bankruptcy procedure in Hong Kong on the premise that the same class of creditors are treated equally.

The Hong Kong administrator shall ensure that the debtor's Hong Kong assets are distributed and paid off to participating Mainland creditors in accordance with Hong Kong insolvency proceeding.

Chapter VIII Cross-border Insolvency

Section 2 Guidelines for Overseas Work of Domestic Administrators

Article 329 Apply to a court of competent jurisdiction

If the debtor's main property is located overseas, has a place of business overseas, or has a representative office overseas, after the People's Court accepts the bankruptcy application, the administrator may apply to an overseas court with jurisdiction for recognition and assistance of Mainland insolvency proceeding, or may apply to the People's Court accepting bankruptcy case, issuing a letter of request, requesting the overseas court to recognize and assist the Mainland proceeding.

Article 330 Materials for applying for a letter of request issued by the People's Court

When applying for a letter of request issued by the People's Court, the administrator shall submit the following materials:

(i) An application;

(ii) A copy of the judgment document applying for recognition and assistance;

(iii) Photocopies of the manager's certificate and the ID card of the contact person;

(iv) Relevant evidence showing that the debtor's main property is located overseas, has a business place overseas, or has a representative office overseas.

Article 331 Items specified in the application form

The application form should state the following:

(i) The debtor's name, place of registration, and the name, position, domicile, identity document information, communication method, etc. of the debtor's main responsible person known to the administrator;

(ii) The name, domicile, identity information and communication method of the individual administrator, and the name, domicile, license or identity information, and communication method of the institutional administrator;

(iii) The progress and plan of the bankruptcy procedure;

(iv) Matters and reasons for applying for recognition and assistance;

(v) The debtor's known property, business place, representative office and creditors abroad;

(vi) The debtor's overseas litigation and arbitration, as well as the preservation measures and enforcement procedures of the debtor's property;

(vii) Relevant information on bankruptcy proceedings against the debtor in other countries or regions;

(viii) Other matters that should be specified.

Article 332 The scope of the administrator's duties performed overseas

After the domestic insolvency proceeding is recognized and assisted overseas, the administrator shall perform the duties of the administrator locally in accordance with the "Enterprise Bankruptcy Law" and the powers granted by the overseas court.

Article 333 Reporting overseas work in a timely manner

The administrator shall promptly submit a report on the execution of duties overseas to the People's Court.

The report shall list the overseas duties performed by the administrator in terms of work preparation, property takeover, and composition of creditor's rights and debts after the administrator accepts the designation.

Article 334 Assistance of the administrator

The administrator shall assist the People's Court in communicating and cooperating with overseas courts and debtors.

Article 335 Jurisdiction over overseas property litigation

For civil lawsuits related to the debtor's overseas property, the administrator can only bring it to the People's Court that accepts the bankruptcy application. After the People's Court makes an effective judgment, the administrator may apply to the People's Court to issue a letter of request, requesting an overseas court to recognize and enforce the effective judgment.

If an arbitration clause or an arbitration agreement has been concluded between the parties before the bankruptcy application is accepted, the relevant case shall be submitted to the selected institution for arbitration.

Chapter IX Bankruptcy Audit

Section 1 Concept and Scope of Bankruptcy Audit

Article 336 The concept of bankruptcy audit

Bankruptcy audit is based on the relevant provisions of the "Enterprise Bankruptcy Law", using specific audit methods to review and evaluate the authenticity, legality and effectiveness of the debtor's financial income and expenditure, assets and liabilities, and issue a special audit report for bankruptcy cases. Special services for trial and administrator work.

Article 337 Classification of bankruptcy audit

According to different audit purposes, bankruptcy audit is divided into assurance business and consulting business. The assurance business requires the accounting firm to implement and issue a corresponding special report. The consulting business can be completed by a certified public accountant as a manager or by a certified public accountant entrusted by the manager.

Article 338 Scope of bankruptcy audit

The scope of a bankruptcy audit generally includes:

(i) The debtor's property inventory;

(ii) Checking and reviewing bankruptcy claims;

(iii) Audit of specific behaviors;

(iv) Economic calculation.

Chapter IX Bankruptcy Audit

Section 2 Debtor's Property Check

Article 339 Scope of debtor's property check

After taking over the debtor, the administrator shall check the debtor's property and submit a property status check report. The scope of property inspection is all property belonging to the debtor at the time of the bankruptcy application, as well as the property acquired by the debtor after the bankruptcy application is accepted to the end of the bankruptcy procedure.

Article 340 Entrustment of debtor property inventory

If an accounting firm serves as the administrator, the accounting firm serving as the administrator may check the debtor's property and issue an audit report on the property check.

If the administrator is a law firm, a liquidation firm or an individual, the administrator may entrust an accounting firm to conduct an inventory of the debtor's property and issue an audit report on the inventory of the property.

Article 341 Objectives of the debtor's property inspection

The goal of the debtor's property inspection is to comprehensively inspect and verify the debtor's various assets, including the inspection of monetary funds, receivables, physical assets, external investments, and assets leased, lent and externally guaranteed, etc., and form a property inspection and audit report. The People's Court shall provide the basis for hearing bankruptcy cases and the work of administrators.

Article 342 Evidence of debtor's property check

The debtor's property inventory shall obtain the following evidences according to different property forms:

(i) For monetary fund such as cash, bank deposits, and other monetary funds, cash monitoring tables, bank statements, bank confirmation letters, credit reports and other certification materials, as well as third-party payment and composition platforms such as Alipay and WeChat of the debtor should be obtained. Information such as digital currency, wealth management or insurance contracts and accounts, etc.;

(ii) For physical assets such as inventories, fixed assets, and construction in progress, a detailed list of assets with storage location, quantity, status, and nature shall be obtained, inventory checklist, warehouse entry and exit records, ownership certificates, real estate and vehicle registration materials, procurement and construction contracts, agreements, invoices, payment documents, project approval, permit, construction, supervision, acceptance and other documents and other supporting documents, etc.; for real estate development enterprises, they should also obtain pre-sale online signature and record, bank mortgage loan, handover list, sales ledger, price difference details of receivable house area, agreement and implementation of debt repayment with property, information on property rights disputes, etc.;

(iii) For negotiable securities or financial assets, the securities registration and composition institution shall obtain the investigation securities information and supporting documents, etc.;

(iv) For intangible assets such as patents, trademarks, copyrights, franchise rights, land use rights, etc., the certificate of title, cost data and relevant contracts shall be obtained;

(v) For creditors' rights such as accounts receivable, prepaid accounts, and other receivables, a list of creditor's rights assets, contracts, agreements, shipping documents and bank payment documents supporting the creditor's rights, debt collection materials, and letter of confirmation shall be obtained. If litigation or arbitration is involved, legal documents for litigation or arbitration should also be obtained;

(vi) For foreign investment, shareholders' resolutions, capital contribution agreements, articles of association of the invested company, capital contribution certificates, capital contribution certificates, financial statements, audit reports, and profit distribution resolutions of the invested company shall be obtained;

(vii) For other asset items not listed in The Operational Guidlines, you can refer to the Auditing Standards for Chinese Certified Public Accountants No. 1301—Audit Evidence to obtain relevant evidence materials.

When it involves the seizure, mortgage, pledge, lien and other ownership restrictions of the debtor's property, the registration information records or internal file materials of the property rights registration department, the written description of the debtor's relevant personnel, and relevant contracts and agreements should be obtained.

Article 343 Negotiations in the process of checking the debtor's property

When an accounting firm conducts an inventory of the debtor's property, it shall negotiate with the client on the purpose of the entrustment, the responsibilities of the client and the debtor, as well as the responsibilities of the accounting firm, work objectives, time requirements, service fees, report distribution and use and other major matters. When deemed necessary, you can ask the administrator, creditors, debtors and prospective investors for their detailed needs.

The accounting firm shall sign an entrustment agreement with the entrusting party on the basis of negotiation. For the negotiation on matters other than the entrustment agreement, written records such as meeting minutes, memorandum or correspondence may be formed.

Article 344 Debtor's property inventory working paper

The accounting firm shall, in accordance with the requirements of the Auditing Standards for Chinese Certified Public Accountants No. 1131—Auditing Working Papers, prepare and file the bankruptcy property inspection working papers.

Article 345 Debtor's property inventory report

Accounting firms shall comply with the Auditing Standards for Chinese Certified Public Accountants No. 1603—Special Considerations for the Audit of a Single Financial Statement and Specific Elements of Financial Statements, and the Standards for Services Related to Chinese Certified Public Accountants No. 4101—Executing Agreed Procedures on Financial Information Issue relevant special audit reports.

Section 3 Inspection and Review of Bankruptcy Claims

Article 346 Entrustment of bankruptcy credit checkup and review

The inspection and review of bankruptcy claims is the responsibility of the administrator. If an accounting firm serves as the manager, the financial part of the inspection and review of claims will no longer be entrusted to the outside world.

After the following matters are reported to the People's Court for permission, the administrator may entrust an accounting firm to issue a special audit report:

(i) Involving a relatively complicated check on employees' claims or employees having major objections to the manager's investigation and publicity list;

(ii) Due to the complicated situation of bankruptcy claims, the administrator does not have the professional ability to review claims;

(iii) If a non-accounting firm serves as the manager, it is deemed necessary to check with the debtor's book accounts payable in the process of reviewing the creditor's rights.

Article 347 Objectives of the inspection and review of bankruptcy claims

The goal of the bankruptcy credit check and review is to conduct a substantive review of whether the credit is established, the nature of the credit, the amount of the credit and the guarantee on the basis of the declaration materials of the credit, and on the basis of the preliminary formal review, so as to confirm the nature and amount of the credit, and provide the basis for the People's Court in bankruptcy proceedings and management workers.

Article 348 Evidence of bankruptcy credit checkup and review

Bankruptcy claims inspection and review should obtain the following evidence according to different claims:

(i) If the declared claims have not been confirmed by valid legal documents, contracts or agreements related to bankruptcy claims, evidence of contract performance, payment vouchers, bank documents, statements, receipts, receipts or invoices, transactions shall be obtained. Letters, right registration certificates, recovery certificates, tax, provident fund unpaid list, etc.;

(ii) Where the declared creditor's rights have been confirmed by effective legal documents, legal documents and effective notices, application execution acceptance notices or execution rulings, and certificates of the paid portion shall be obtained;

(iii) If there are other debtors for the declared creditor's rights, an explanation of the performance of the other debtors shall be obtained;

(iv) If the declared creditor's rights are secured by property, evidence to prove the property security shall be obtained.

For employees' creditor's rights that do not need to be declared, they shall obtain the roster of employees, registration form, identification certificate, labor contract, social security registration certificate or wage distribution form, list of wages owed to employees and expenses for medical treatment, disability allowance and pension, and payment records printed by tax, social security and provident fund departments.

Article 349 Negotiation in the process of checking and reviewing bankruptcy claims

The inspection and review of bankruptcy claims mainly involves negotiation with administrators, creditors, debtors and employees. The accounting firm shall negotiate with the client on such major matters as the purpose of the entrustment, the responsibilities of the client and the debtor, and the responsibilities of the accounting firm, work objectives, time requirements, service fees, and responsibilities for the distribution and use of reports.

The accounting firm shall sign an entrustment agreement with the client on the basis of negotiation. For the negotiation on matters other than the entrustment agreement, written records such as meeting minutes, memorandum or correspondence may be formed.

Article 350 Working papers for inventory and review of bankruptcy claims

The accounting firm shall, with reference to the requirements of the Auditing Standards for Chinese Certified Public Accountants No. 1131-Auditing Working Papers, prepare and file the bankruptcy creditor's rights inventory and review working papers.

Article 351 Bankruptcy credit checkup and review report

Auditing and auditing of bankruptcy claims by accounting firms shall comply with the Auditing Standards for Chinese Certified Public Accountants No. 1603—Special Considerations for Auditing of Single Financial Statements and Specific Elements of Financial Statements, and the Standards for Services Related to Chinese Certified Public Accountants No. 4101-Implementing the Agreed Procedures for Financial Information, etc., and issuing special inspection or audit reports.

The accounting firm may accept the entrustment of the administrator to prepare the "Debt Statement" on behalf of the administrator in accordance with the requirements of the "China Certified Public Accountants Related Service Standards No. 4111 - Compiling Financial Information" and the "Enterprise Bankruptcy Law".

Section 4 Specific Behavior Audit

Article 352 Concept of audit of specific conduct

The specific conduct audit is, based on Articles 31, 32, 33, 35 and 36 of the Enterprise Bankruptcy Law, audit the revocable behavior, individual liquidation behavior, invalid behavior, shareholder's capital contribution behavior, abnormal income and usurpation behavior of debtor's directors, supervisors and senior management personnel.

Article 353 Delegation of audit of specified behaviors

If an accounting firm serves as the manager, the accounting firm serving as the manager may conduct an audit of specific behaviors and issue a special audit report on specific behaviors.

If the administrator is a law firm, a liquidation firm or an individual, the administrator shall entrust an accounting firm to conduct an audit of specific behaviors and issue a special audit report for specific behaviors.

Article 354 Objectives of specific conduct audits

The objective of the specific behavior audit is to audit the facts of specific behaviors involving the debtor's property stipulated in the "Enterprise Bankruptcy Law", and provide a basis for the administrator to collect the debtor's property, recover economic losses, and protect the interests of creditors.

Article 355 Evidence of audit of specific conduct

Specific conduct audits should obtain the following evidence depending on the nature of the audit:

(i) For revocable acts involving the debtor's property within one year before accepting the bankruptcy application, the financial write-off certificate, asset transfer contract, transfer pricing basis documents, new property guarantee contract, debt repayment certificate, etc. shall be obtained;

(ii) For revocable individual repayment actions within six months before accepting the bankruptcy application, the debt repayment certificate, the accounting certificate for the occurrence of the debt and the relevant contract agreement shall be obtained. At the same time, check whether the debtor's property is benefited from the individual repayment;

(iii) For the invalid act of concealing or transferring property and fictitious debts or accepting untrue debts, the financial write-off and asset transfer certificates, financial write-up and transfer-to-add liabilities certificates, relevant contracts and agreements, compositions, letters of entrustment, etc. shall be obtained;

(iv) For the capital contribution that the debtor's capital contributor has not performed or fully performed, the capital contribution agreement, the company's articles of association, the accounting certificate of the debtor's paid-in shareholder's capital contribution, the bank's running water or bank's receipt certificate of the debtor's paid-in shareholder's capital contribution, and the shareholders of each stage shall be obtained. Capital verification report of capital contribution, approval document of non-monetary property capital contribution, relevant assessment report of physical asset capital contribution, property ownership certification document, ownership change registration document, other shareholders' determination of the shareholder's physical capital contribution value, etc.;

(v) For the debtor's directors, supervisors, and senior managers' abnormal income and misappropriation of the debtor's property, the debtor's remuneration management system, employee salary tables, bank records for the payment of executive remuneration, funds transaction records between the debtor and senior managers, and accounting vouchers, transaction records and accounting vouchers of the debtor and senior management personnel should be obtained.

Article 356 Consultation in the process of auditing specific acts

The specific behavior audit mainly involves negotiation with the entrusting party, the debtor and the debtor's shareholders, managers, etc. The accounting firm shall consult with the client on the purpose of the entrustment, the responsibilities of the client and the debtor, as well as the responsibilities of the accounting firm, work objectives, time requirements, service fees, and responsibilities for the distribution and use of reports.

The accounting firm shall sign an entrustment agreement with the entrusting party on the basis of negotiation. For the negotiation on matters other than the entrustment agreement, written records such as meeting minutes, memorandum or correspondence may be formed.

Article 357 Specific conduct audit working papers

Accounting firms shall, in accordance with the requirements of Auditing Standards for Chinese Certified Public Accountants No. 1131-Auditing Working Papers, prepare and file auditing working papers for specific behaviors.

Article 358 Specific conduct audit report

Accounting firms shall comply with the Auditing Standards for Chinese Certified Public Accountants No. 1603—Special Considerations for the Audit of a Single Financial Statement and Specific Elements of Financial Statements, and the Standards for Services Related to Chinese Certified Public Accountants No. 4101—Executing Agreed Procedures on Financial Information Issue relevant special audit reports.

The audit of specific behaviors completed by an accounting firm as an administrator may not submit a special audit report, but shall be recorded in the form of an administrator's document.

Section 5 Economic Calculation

Article 359 Matters of economic calculation

When the administrator encounters the following matters in the process of executing bankruptcy affairs, it shall make economic calculations:

(i) Rescind or continue to perform the contract;

(ii) Continue or stop the business of the debtor;

(iii) Comparison of debt composition ratios between reorganization and liquidation;

(iv) Feasibility analysis of the draft reorganization plan;

(v) Feasibility analysis of the draft composition agreement;

(vi) Other economic decision-making matters in bankruptcy proceedings.

Article 360 Entrustment of economic estimates

Economic measurement is the responsibility of the administrator. When the administrator is held by an accounting firm or an individual certified public accountant, professional institutions are no longer entrusted. If the manager is not an accounting firm or an individual certified public accountant, and the manager does not have the professional measurement ability, he may entrust an accounting firm or other professional organization to conduct special economic measurement.

The accounting firm shall sign the entrustment agreement in the name of the accounting firm after confirming that it has the professional competence for the entrusted matters.

Article 361 Objectives of economic calculations

The goal of economic calculation is to draw conclusions on economic benefits through quantitative calculation or certain financial analysis, and provide a basis for People's Courts to try bankruptcy cases or administrators to make decisions.

Article 362 Evidence of economic calculation

Economic calculations should obtain the following evidence based on different economic events:

(i) The debtor's business information, including the brand of products or services, market position, industry environment and development stage, reasons for business deterioration, business data, upstream and downstream relationships, etc.;

(ii) The debtor's financial information, including accounting statements, ledger, account books, vouchers, audit reports, evaluation reports, consulting reports, etc.;

(iii) Property valuation and realization forecast, including asset appraisal report, online inquiry report, relevant expert opinions, relevant transaction cases disclosed in the market, etc.;

(iv) The corresponding policies of the human resources and social security department, and the standards for employee remuneration and recompositing fees;

(v) The debtor's contractual agreement, creditor's rights and debt certificates, relevant litigation materials, etc. on the economic matters that need to be measured.

Article 363 Negotiation of economic estimates

When an accounting firm accepts an entrustment to provide economic measurement services, it shall communicate with the client about the purpose of the entrustment, the responsibilities of the client and the debtor, and the responsibilities of the accounting firm, work objectives, time requirements, service fees, and responsibilities for the distribution and use of reports. When the accounting firm deems necessary, it can understand the detailed needs of managers, creditors, debtors and prospective investors.

The accounting firm shall sign an entrustment agreement with the entrusting party on the basis of negotiation. For the negotiation on matters other than the entrustment agreement, written records such as meeting minutes, memorandum or correspondence may be formed.

Article 364 Working papers for economic calculations

The provision of economic measurement services by accounting firms is an agreed procedure. According to the requirements of the "China Certified Public Accountants Related Service Standards No. 4101-Implementing Agreed Procedures for Financial Information", the major matters supporting the business report of the agreed procedures should be recorded and the evidence of the execution of agreed procedures in accordance with the provisions of this Code and the requirements of the delegation agreement should be recorded. When compiling the working papers, you can refer to the "China Certified Public Accountants Auditing Standards No. 1131-Auditing Working Papers".

Article 365 Economic calculation report

When an accounting firm accepts an entrustment to conduct economic calculations, it shall submit a special report to the client on the work results formed. The content of the report shall be implemented with reference to "China Certified Public Accountants Related Service Standards No. 4101-Implementing Agreed Procedures for Financial Information".

The economic measurement business completed by an accounting firm as an administrator may not submit a special report, but shall be recorded in the form of an administrator's document.

Chapter X Bankruptcy-Related Tax Matters

Article 366 Administrator's tax work

The debtor's taxation work mainly includes notifying the tax authority to declare the creditor's rights, applying for the issuance of invoices or applying for the issuance of invoices as required and properly managed, tax declaration, liquidation declaration, removal of abnormal status, application of preferential tax policies, application for tax credit restoration, tax cancellation, etc.

Article 367 Entrustment of tax affairs

When necessary, the administrator can entrust professional tax personnel or institutions to handle the tax-related affairs of the bankrupt debtor.

Article 368 Handover of tax information

When taking over the debtor's tax information, the administrator should pay attention to handing over the tax control equipment, business login account and password, Ukey, unused VAT invoices, and the contact information of the tax administrator.

Article 369 Tax declaration

The administrator conducts tax returns, which generally include:

(i) Daily tax declaration: personal income tax, value-added tax, real estate tax, land use tax, enterprise income tax, etc.;

(ii) Tax declaration of property disposal: value-added tax, enterprise income tax, stamp duty, etc.;

(iii) Tax declaration at the end of the liquidation period: enterprise income tax, etc.;

(iv) Tax declaration during bankruptcy and reorganization: application and application of preferential tax policies, etc.;

(v) Tax declaration during bankruptcy composition: application and application of preferential tax policies, etc.

Article 370 Tax cancellation

When the People's Court decides to declare the debtor bankrupt, the administrator shall formulate the legal procedures and various work plans for implementing the debtor's tax clearance and other bankruptcy liquidation procedures.

The administrator shall formulate the time plan and arrangement for the tax cancellation work before implementing the tax cancellation work, so as to ensure that the tax cancellation work is carried out in an orderly manner and completed on time.

Before the administrator applies for tax deregistration, if there are unfinished tax-related matters, the administrator needs to complete the tax deregistration first and then apply for tax deregistration.

Chapter XI Supplementary Provisions

Article 371 Documentary materials

The documents issued by the administrators when performing their duties shall be prepared in accordance with the documents issued by the People's Courts.

Article 372 Administrator work platform

The administrator shall use the administrator's work platform to disclose case information in accordance with the requirements of the "Supreme People's Court Enterprise Bankruptcy Case Administrator's Work Platform Use Measures (Trial)" and the "Supreme People's Court Enterprise Bankruptcy Case Information Disclosure Regulations (Trial)".

Article 373 Interpretation

These Operational Guidelines are explained by the Guangdong Association of Bankruptcy Administrators.

Article 374 Effective Date

These Operational Guidelines is promulgated on November 26, 2021, and effective as of on the date of promulgation.

www.ingramcontent.com/pod-product-compliance
Lightning Source LLC
Chambersburg PA
CBHW080412230426
43662CB00016B/2379